Royal English Bookbindings

Cyril Davenport

Alpha Editions

This edition published in 2023

ISBN : 9789357941013

Design and Setting By
Alpha Editions
www.alphaedis.com
Email - info@alphaedis.com

Contents

PROLOGUE

It is curious that twice in English history the royal libraries have been given to the nation. The ancient royal collection, containing manuscripts from the reign of Richard III., was added to by each sovereign in turn; but it seems to have been brought into notice and taken special care of by Prince Henry, the eldest son of James I. Out of his own private income, this Prince added largely to the old collection, and purchased the important libraries of Lord Lumley, of a Welshman named Maurice, and that of Isaac Casaubon. On his death the library became the property of James I., and after some other changes, both the old library and that of Prince Henry were deposited at Ashburnham House, where in 1731 there was a fire which damaged some of it. It was then removed to the old Dormitory at Westminster, and in 1757 it was presented by George II. to the nation, and was handed over to the Trustees of the Sloane and Cottonian Libraries, and placed in Montagu House, then newly purchased as a National Museum. There were at this time in the old royal library about 15,000 volumes altogether, and very many of them were still in their ancient and beautiful bindings.

George III., finding on his accession to the throne that there was no royal library, very energetically set to work to form a new collection. He chose his agents very carefully, and appointed Sir Frederick Barnard to be his librarian. Sir Frederick travelled widely in search of books, and, acting partly under the advice of Dr. Samuel Johnson, eventually brought together perhaps the finest collection of books ever made by one man. On the king's death the library contained upwards of 65,000 volumes, besides more than 19,000 separate tracts and some manuscripts.

Generally speaking, the bindings in the "King's Library"—the name by which George III.'s collection is now known in the British Museum—are modern; but among them are a considerable number of old bindings in good condition, and it is possible that those which were rebound were mostly in a bad state. Unfortunately the crowned monogram of George III. is generally impressed in a prominent place, even on such old bindings as have been otherwise preserved intact; and although valuable as a record it is often a great disfigurement. There is little doubt that George III.'s intention was to create a new royal library to remain in the possession of the kings themselves, but there seems to have been some idea that it would eventually become national property, as Dr. Frederick Wendeborn, a German preacher, well known at Court, wrote: "The King's Private Library ... can boast very valuable and magnificent books, which, as it is said, will at one time or another be joined to those of the British Museum." This prediction was fulfilled in 1823, when George IV. presented it to the nation, and the fine room now known as the King's Library in the British Museum was built for its reception, the removal being completed in 1828.

William IV. does not seem to have been altogether pleased that the royal libraries should have been twice given away, as he added a codicil to his will in 1833, bequeathing to the Crown "all his additions to the libraries in the several royal palaces," with an autograph confirmation dated from Brighton, November 30, 1834, signed and sealed by himself, declaring "that all the books, drawings, and plans collected in all the palaces shall for ever continue heirlooms to the Crown, and on no pretence whatever to be alienated from the Crown."

The royal library at Windsor now contains the greatest number of royal bindings now existing in any one collection, except those at the British Museum, but it possesses very few that belonged to Tudor sovereigns. From the time of James I. it has a very fine collection.

Where I have not specifically mentioned otherwise, the books described in the following pages are in the British Museum. They should be to the English people especially interesting, for not only are they national property, but any of them can be seen with little trouble, and a considerable number are actually exhibited in the binding show-cases in the King's Library, or in the Grenville Library.

CHAPTER I

The rulers of England and of France have, ever since the introduction of printing into Europe, been great patrons of books, and moreover have by their individual tastes, both literary and artistic, largely influenced the styles of bookbinding prevalent during their reigns.

In England from the time of Henry VII. onwards, and in France from Louis XII., a noble series of royal bookbindings exists at the present time, and may be considered with justice to be typical of the best work done at the different periods. Although there are a few great binders who do not appear, as far as is at present known, to have worked for royalty, there is no doubt that most of the great masters of this most fascinating art were at some time or other privileged to work for the sovereign houses of their time, if indeed they were not actually royal binders.

Before printing was introduced into England in the fifteenth century by William Caxton, there is little or no record of any special collection of books made by any English sovereign. It is possible no such collection ever was made, but if it were, all trace and record of it is now lost. Rich mediæval bindings of a decorative character, such as are not uncommon in other countries, are unknown in England, and it is supposed that, for the sake of the valuable metal and gems which were commonly used on such bindings, they were destroyed under the early Tudor kings. At the same time, it seems unlikely that Henry VIII. or Edward VI. would have pulled to pieces any fine bindings, if they had already formed part of a royal library.

It is difficult in the case of antiquities, the full record of which is not forthcoming, to be sure of statements which may be made concerning them; but so many antiquaries and men of mark have already borne testimony at all events to the probable truth of the legend that the coronation book of Henry I. still exists, that I feel any record of English royal bookbindings would be imperfect, not only without mention of it, but even without a detailed description. I think, however, that without exception every other book I shall describe or mention has upon it, or in it, some absolute mark of royal ownership, but on the other hand they are all much later. Indeed, as far as I know, no book of the twelfth century has any mark of ownership upon it, although the makers' name does rarely occur.

The book in question (Plate I.) is quite small, measuring 7 × 4½ inches. It is a manuscript on vellum of lessons from the four gospels in Latin, written in the twelfth century; it also contains the whole of the Gospel of St. John except a small portion missing, and some other MSS. The binding is of thick wooden boards, covered probably with deer-skin. The lower cover has a sunk panel, and bears a crucified figure of our Lord cast in bronze, finely chased and formerly gilt. The corners are guarded with bossed pieces of brass, stamped with a device of a fleur-de-lis within a circle, and there is a clasp of leather and brass. The figure of our Lord appears distinctly old, but the rest of the metal work has not such evidence of antiquity, and it seems likely that it is much more recent. Inside the book are several manuscript notes by various owners, the most interesting of which is signed by John Ives, at "Yarmouth, St. Luke's Day, 1772." He says this "appears to be the original book on which our Kings and Queens took their coronation oaths before the Reformation." In Powell's *Repertoire of Records*, 1631, at p. 123, he mentions "a little booke with a crucifix" as being preserved in the chest of the King's Remembrancer at the Exchequer.

Mr. Thomas Martin of Palgrave, owner of the book in the beginning of the eighteenth century, at one time lent it to Mr. Thomas Madox, author of the *History of the Exchequer*, and his opinion was that it was the book formerly belonging to the Exchequer, mentioned by Powell, and which was used to take the coronation oath upon by all our kings and queens till Henry VIII.

It belonged afterwards to Mr. Thomas Astle, F.S.A., Keeper of the Records in the Tower of London, who died in 1803, and whose library was purchased by the Marquis of Buckingham and kept at Stowe in a beautiful Gothic room specially built for it. In June 1849 the library became the property of Lord Ashburnham, and from him it was purchased in 1883 by the Trustees of the British Museum, excepting the Irish MSS., which went to Dublin. This collection is now known as the Stowe Collection.

There is a drawing of this book by Mr. George Vertue, presented by him to the Society of Antiquaries and still preserved in their library.

From the time of Henry I. until that of Edward IV. there is no trace of any English royal bindings, and then only a small one. There is in the library of Westminster Abbey a loose leather binding impressed with a panel-stamp of the arms of Edward IV., crowned and supported by the two white lions of the Earls of March, and, moreover, at the top the two angels which are afterwards often found on the larger panel-stamps of a similar kind used in the time of Henry VIII. No other binding exists apparently that belonged to Edward IV., even if this one did, but in the wardrobe accounts of his reign are found several notices of binding. One reads, "for binding, gilding, and dressing" of books, but does not say what the material is. It was probably leather, calf or goat, as gilding on velvet does not seem to have then been thought of, although the material itself was certainly used, as in another place it is stated that "velvet vj yerdes cremysy figured" were delivered for the covering of the books of our lord the king; and indeed it is curious if the "gilding" was applied even to leather, as certainly no instances are known at so early a date of English origin.

Actual instances of the use of velvet for bookbinding occur first among the books of Henry VII. and Henry VIII., and the value, beauty, and wonderful durability of it are likely enough to have attracted the notice of royal and learned book lovers.

Henry VII. was the first of our kings whose literary tastes have left any mark on our existing collections. He acquired a magnificent series of volumes printed on vellum at Paris by Antoine Verard, a celebrated French printer, besides other valuable books. This collection is now at the British Museum almost complete, and it is rebound in velvet. It is likely that the original binding was also velvet, but record of it is lost. There is, however, one magnificent volume that fortunately was so splendid and in so fine a condition that the ruthless rebinder has spared it. This is a copy of the Indentures made between Henry VII. and John Islippe, Abbot of Westminster, for the foundation of the chantrey. It is written on vellum, and its counterpart is preserved in the Public Record Office.

It is covered in crimson velvet, edged with gold cord, and having tassels of crimson silk and gold, the velvet projecting broadly over the edges. On each side are centre and corner bosses of silver, gilt and enamelled. The centre bosses bear the royal coat-of-arms wrought in high relief, with the supporters used by the king—the red dragon of his ancestor Cadwallader, and the white greyhound he used both by right of his wife through the Nevills and his own maternal ancestors the Earls of Somerset. The corner bosses bear the portcullis, the emblem of the castle of Beaufort in Anjou, the residence of Catherine Swinford, and where Henry's maternal grandfather was born. Each of these portcullises is borne upon a white and green ground, the livery colours of the Tudors, and it has been used as a royal badge from the time of Henry VII. until the present day.

The book is held together by bands of gold braid, and fastened by beautiful clasps of richly-chased silver-gilt, with enamelled red roses. Appended to the boards are five impressions of the Great Seal, each in a silver box, with either a portcullis or a red rose upon it. The seals hang by plaited cords of green and gold.

There are similar books of Henry VII.'s besides this one. A fine instance was shown at the Burlington Fine Arts Club Exhibition of Binding in 1891. It is a *Book of Penalties for non-performance of services in the Chapel of Henry VII. at Westminster*, and is bound in red velvet, with tassels and silver-gilt and enamelled bosses like those just described. It has silver clasps, and four silver boxes containing the seals of the parties to the indenture depend from the lower edge.

FIG. 1.—*Indentures between Henry VII, and John Islippe,
Abbot of Westminster, concerning the foundation
of the Chantrey, etc., MS.*

On one book, probably once the property of Henry VII., which somehow became separated from the rest, is found his coat-of-arms impressed on the gilt edges—a curious and early instance of decorative edge-work. A drawing of it was published in *Bibliographica*, vol. ii. p. 395. It is a Sarum Missal, Rouen, 1497, and was given to Cardinal Pole probably by Queen Mary, and eventually purchased by the British Museum.

Henry VIII. apparently thought much of his library and its proper preservation and extension. He appointed John Leland, the antiquary, to be his library keeper, and gave him a special commission under the Broad Seal to travel and collect all kinds of antiquities and make records of them. Leland acquired, under these powers, many valuable manuscripts from the monasteries, then so ruthlessly being despoiled of their treasures; but, unfortunately, he does not seem to have been able to preserve any of the precious bindings in which many of them were doubtless encased.

There is a considerable amount of documentary evidence concerning the binding of Henry VIII.'s books. Notices occur in the records of the "Privy Purse Expenses" of payments for velvet and vellum; and these two materials are again largely mentioned in the most interesting account now preserved among the additional manuscripts at the British Museum of the royal printer and binder, "Thomas Berthelett." This account, which is very full, refers to work done during the years 1541-43; and although, so far, no actual book has been identified as being one of those mentioned, yet the bindings we still possess of Henry VIII.'s are so generally of the same kind as those described that there seems little doubt that most, if not all of them, were bound by Berthelet.

He mentions a Psalter "covered with crimosyn satyne," and we possess a collection of tracts bound in this manner, with a delicate tracery of gold cord, and on the edges is written in gold the words "REX IN ÆTERNUM VIVE NEEZ." This is probably what Berthelet, in an entry a little further on, calls "drawyng in gold on the transfile." There are several mentions of books "gorgiously gilded on the leather," and also others where he says books are bound "backe to backe" none of which seem to have survived, but there are plenty of instances of the "white leather gilt," so often used. "Purple velvet" was used to cover "ij Primers," which are now lost; but we possess a splendid volume covered in this way with embroidery upon it, and again he says he has bound books after the "Venecian fascion" and "Italian fascion." Truly the Italian work of the late fifteenth and early sixteenth centuries is extremely fine, and Berthelet may have seen some specimens of it, and, admiring them, have endeavoured to imitate their peculiar and beautiful gilded tooling.

To Berthelet must be conceded the honour of being the first English binder to use gold stamped work on leather, and he does so with admirable effect. Many of his bindings gilded on white leather, sometimes deer-skin, sometimes vellum, are most charming; indeed, the taste for vellum has never died out in England from Berthelet's time to the present day, when we have William Morris's dainty volumes with their green ties. Berthelet's books also generally had ties, but they are now all worn off.

A fine instance of this white leather and gold occurs on Sir Thomas Elyot's *Image of Governance*, printed by Berthelet in 1541.

It bears the same design on each side. A panel, enclosed by an ornamental fillet, contains a very graceful arrangement of curves forming a central space in which are the words "Dieu et mon Droit"; and at each side of this the royal initials contained in two semicircles left for them. At each of the inner corners is a large set stamp, and the ground is dotted over with small circles and the daisy—a badge used by the Tudors probably as a compliment to their ancestress Margaret de Beaufort. On the edges are painted in gold the words "REX IN ÆTERNUM VIVE."

Some of the same stamps are used on another book which is probably Berthelet's work. It is a manuscript Latin commentary on the campaign of the Emperor Charles V. against the French in 1544, addressed by Anthonius de Musica to Henry VIII. It is bound in brown calf, and bears within a broad outer fillet a panel containing in the centre the royal coat-of-arms and initials enclosed in an inner rectangular panel; above and below this are two rectangular cartouches, with titles of the king and various initials which have not yet been interpreted. Flanking the long central panel are medallions of Plato and Dido, favourite stamps afterwards with English binders, but occurring here for the first time.

A design which was probably a favourite one of Berthelet's is found on a copy of *Opus eximium de vera differentia Regiæ Potestatis et Ecclesiasticæ*, printed by him in 1534 (Fig. 2). There is an instance of the same binding in the Bodleian Library at Oxford. The arms of the king, with the supporters of the dragon and the greyhound, occupy the centre of each board. This is enclosed in an oval ribbon bearing the words "Rex Henricus VIII. Dieu et mon Droit," and the whole is surrounded by an ornamental fillet with decorative corners. Above and below the shield are crowned double roses and the initials K. H.

A collection of sixteenth-century tracts is covered with crimson satin, and ornamented with an arabesque design outlined in gold cord. This is the earliest English book remaining that is bound in satin, but no doubt many more existed, as they are so often mentioned in accounts of the time. The satin is always crimson, and, curiously enough, long afterwards under the Stuarts the use of satin was revived, but of a white colour. This collection of tracts was certainly enough bound for the king, as it has the peculiarity of the motto painted on its edges in gold, "REX IN ÆTERNUM VIVE NEEZ," which seems to have been a favourite form of decoration of Berthelet's, so very likely this is one of his books.

Velvet, mentioned also by Berthelet, is used to cover a large Bible printed at Zurich in 1543, but there does not appear very clearly any mark by which it can be identified as his work. It is now of a tawny colour, but was originally probably crimson, and on it is outlined an elaborate design in gold cord. A broad outer border has an arabesque pattern arranged diamond-wise, with large double roses at each corner. Within this is a smaller rectangular border, enclosing a circle with the king's initials bound together by a scroll, and above and below the circle a repeating arabesque design. On the edges of this book are very elaborate heraldic paintings.

A different kind of work altogether covers the splendid *Description de toute la terre Sainte*, by Martin de Brion (Fig. 3), a beautiful manuscript on vellum dedicated to Henry VIII., and full of illuminated reference to him and his heraldic attributes.

It is bound in purple velvet and richly embroidered, and is the first of a splendid series of embroidered books on velvet executed in England. The design is simple, but it is carried out with such skill and taste that it is altogether most effective. In the centre is the royal coat-of-arms, the coats of France and England quarterly, as borne by our sovereigns from Richard II. to Elizabeth, Edward III., who first used the French coat, having originally borne it *semée de fleurs-de-lis*, but the number of these having been reduced to three by Charles VI. of France, a corresponding change was made in the English coat by his son-in-law Richard.

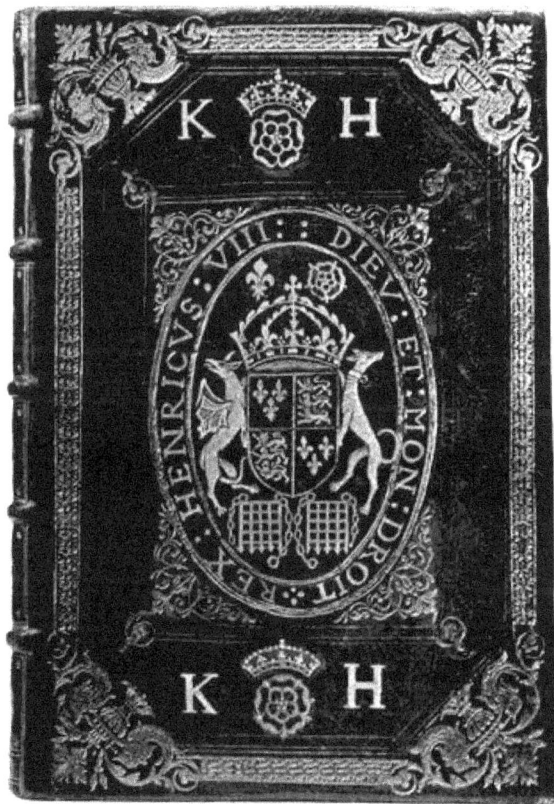

FIG. 2.—*Opus eximium de vera differentia Regiæ Potestatis et Ecclesiasticæ. Londini, 1534. Henry VIII.*

The bearings on these coats are worked in gold thread on a couched groundwork of silk of the proper colours. The coat is ensigned by a large royal crown worked in gold thread, freely adorned with pearls on the arches, the crosses, and the fleurs-de-lis, as also on the rim, which is further ornamented with "jewels" of coloured silks. The blue Garter, with its motto in gold, and the spaces between the words marked by small red roses, surrounds the coat. The king's initial H.'s, originally worked in seed pearls, but now only showing the threads, flank the central design, and the corners are filled with raised Lancastrian roses of red silk, appliqués, and finished with gold.

There is still another kind of binding used for one of the volumes in the British Museum that was made for Henry VIII., and that is of gold. It is a tiny copy of a metrical version of the penitential and other Psalms in English by John Cheke, Clerk in Chancery, written on vellum early in the sixteenth century (Plate II.) It has at the beginning a miniature portrait of Henry VIII., and is bound in gold, worked in open-leaf tracery, with remains of black enamel on many of the leaves and on the border surrounding them. The panels of the back have each a small pattern cut into the metal, and filled with a black enamel. At the top of each cover is a small ring so that the volume could be attached to the girdle. It is said to have been given by Queen Anne Boleyn when on the scaffold to one of her maids of honour, and it now forms part of the Stowe Collection at the British Museum.

Penitential Psalms, etc., MS., sixteenth century. Gold Binding. Henry VIII.

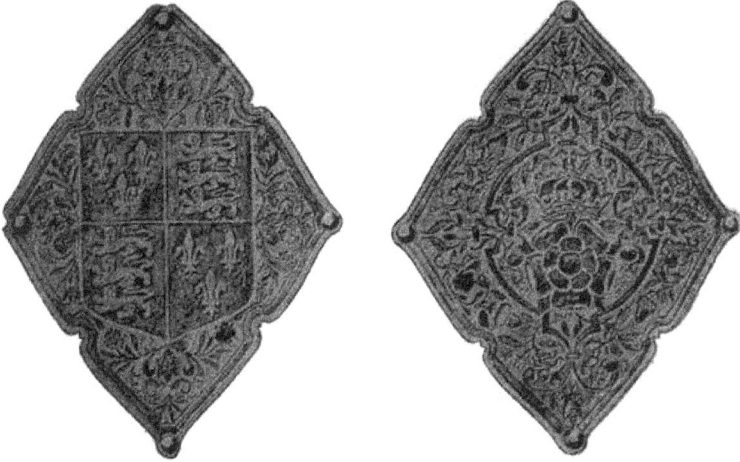

Novum Testamentum Græce. Lutetiæ, 1550. Gold centres. Queen Elizabeth.

A book curiously decorated and bound in calf for Henry VIII. is a Bible printed at Antwerp in 1534, and in two volumes. These are large books measuring 14½ × 9 inches, and both of them have been restored at the outer edges. The inner panel, rectangular with large corners, encloses on each side sentences in French, above and below which are crowned double roses and the initials H. A., probably standing for "Henry" and "Anna." The sentence reads on one side, "AINSI QUE TOUS MEURENT PAR ADAM," and on the other, "AUSSY TOUS SERONT VIVIFIES PAR CHRIST." The borders and corners are very rich and decorative, and it is likely that the outer ornamentation, although it is actually modern, has been carefully copied from the original.

A handsome binding in dark brown calf covers an "old royal" manuscript, *Jul. Claud Iguini oratio ad Hen. VIII.*, written probably about 1540. It has blind and gold lines, and the design is an outer border with an arabesque pattern stamped in gold, enclosing the royal coat-of-arms, crowned, and enclosed within a Garter. Round this again are four Greek words, "ΠΛΙΟΣ ΠΑΝΤΑΣ ΑΛΙΕΝΩΝ ΕΞΑΡΚΤΟΝ," the meaning of which is not clear. On the coat-of-arms it is notable that the three lions of England are crowned. This peculiarity occurs sometimes in other books, but I believe heraldically the lions should not be crowned, and this book is the earliest instance I have met with in which they are so shown.

FIG. 3.—*Description of the Holy Land, in French.*
By Martin Brion. MS. Henry VIII.

Galteri Deloeni Libellus de tribus Hierarchiis, a manuscript dedicated to Henry and probably bound by Thomas Berthelet, is one of his most decorative bindings on a small book (Plate III.) The design is simple, a rectangle and a diamond fillet interlaced, enclosing the royal coat-of-arms crowned. In the two lower spaces below the shield are the crucifixion and the serpent in the wilderness with their corresponding texts, and the rest of the spaces are very fully filled with small stamps of arabesques, double roses, single and double daisies, stars, and leaves. The execution of the actual gilding is coarse, and the finish generally is not as perfect as it might be, but the general effect is excellent.

One of the most interesting bindings of any that were made for Henry VIII. is that which was, or is supposed to have been, worked for him by his daughter Elizabeth. It is part of the old royal library in the British Museum, and is written on vellum in the Princess's own most careful and precise handwriting. It is a collection of prayers composed by Queen Katharine Parr, and translated by Elizabeth into Latin, French, and Italian, and dated "Hereford, December 20, 1545." The dedication is, "Illustrissimo Henrico octavo, Anglie, Francie, Hiberniæq. regi, fidei defensori." The volume is quite small, 5¾ inches by 4, and is covered in red silk, with a gold thread in it, woven with a very large mesh, or even possibly made by hand. In the centre of each board is a large monogram worked in a thick cord of blue silk, through which runs a silver thread. The monogram, like so many similar arrangements of letters, causes much difference of opinion among the experts who endeavour to interpret it. My solution is that it is composed of the letters "A. F. H. REX," the meaning of which is "Anglie, Francie, Hiberniæque Rex," in accordance with the words used by Elizabeth in her dedication, and the two H's, worked in a thick red silk cord with a silver thread in it, which are above and below the monogram, supply the needful name. I do not know that this interpretation is by any one considered to be the right one, but it appears to me at all events as plausible as any of the others I have heard. At each corner is a heartsease of purple and gold and small green leaves. This most curious and interesting binding is in many ways nearly allied to that made for Queen Katharine Parr, which is now at the Bodleian Library at Oxford, and which I shall presently describe. This binding is also considered to be the work of the Princess Elizabeth, and I think that the similarity in the peculiar groundwork, the identity of the pansies in the corners, and the use of braid or very thick thread in each, producing a maximum of effect with a minimum of labour, are all strong reasons for believing that both volumes are the work of the same hand, namely, that, of the Princess herself.

Deloenus. Libellus de tribus Hierarchiis, etc., MS. Henry VIII.

The Bodleian binding is in very fair condition, but the British Museum one is, unfortunately, in a very dilapidated state. Luckily, however, it has not been restored, so what is left can be safely examined and relied upon.

English royal bindings, of old date especially, now rarely come into the open market, but in the latter part of last year a most interesting specimen that belonged to Henry VIII. was purchased by the British Museum. It is a manuscript on the science of geometry, written on paper and dedicated to the king. It is bound in white leather, and has many signs that it is the work of Thomas Berthelet. There is an outer border of blind and gold lines, with solid arabesques at the outer corners, and stars in the inner corners. The centre of each board bears a geometrical design of triangles and lines filled in with stars and dots. In the upper part of each board is a cartouche bearing the words "VIVAT REX," and at the lower part a similar cartouche with the word "GEOMETRIA," followed by an arabesque ornament. Written in gold on the white edges are the words "REX IN ÆTERNUM VIVE NEEZ." There is no book of Berthelet's, except this one, on which the decoration has any reference to the contents of the volume. It is indeed probable that this is actually one of the first books in which there has been any endeavour to make the outside decoration agree with the subject-matter inside.

The word "Nez," or "Neez," which usually occurs after the "Rex in Æternum Vive" so frequently painted on the edges of Henry VIII.'s books, has been a puzzle for some time. Mr. E. L. Scott of the British Museum suggests that it may stand for the first letters of the words "Ναβουχοδονόσωρ ἐσαεὶ ζῆθι," as the king to whom the words are addressed in the Book of Daniel is Nebuchadnezzar. This explanation I have already given in *Bibliographica*, part viii.

In the sixteenth century in England a great many books were decorated in what is called "blind," that is to say, without the use of gold-leaf, with large panel-stamps. Two of these stamps bear the royal coat-of-arms, with supporters ensigned with the crown. The larger of them has above the crown a double rose and two angels bearing scrolls, and dependent from the shield, by chains, are two portcullises. The smaller and inferior stamp has, in the upper portion, representations of the sun and moon, with usually the Cross of St. George and the arms of the City of London. The first of these stamps may, I think, have been originally cut for the king's own use; but the second is undoubtedly a trade stamp. The signification of it probably is, that the binder who used it was a Freeman of the City of London. I have given figures of these designs in the *Queen* of June 20, 1891, in illustration of a paper on early London bookbindings. The stamp with the angels is often used in conjunction with the stamps of Katharine of Arragon and Anne Boleyn, to be hereafter described; and I mention it here because it is not at all uncommon, and is very generally supposed to be actually royal, but, as far as I have been able to ascertain, there is no instance of its use upon a book which is known to have been so, and now it is generally considered to be only a trade stamp. In judging stamps of this kind, it must not be forgotten that they were cut in hard metal and only used on soft leather, so that they would last a very long time indeed. Generally, some other evidence of the ownership of the book should be adduced beyond a mere existence of a single stamp.

For Katharine of Arragon a large panel-stamp was cut bearing her coat-of-arms impaled with that of England, crowned, and having two angels as supporters. An example of this occurs on a copy of *Whittington, De octo partibus orationis*, London, 1521. On the other side of the book is the large stamp of the king's arms already described. A similar stamp was used with the substitution of the arms of Queen Anne Boleyn for those of Queen Katharine. There is now no instance of the use of either of these stamps on a royal book.

George Vertue, in his notes on the Fine Arts, says that small gold books were given to Queen Anne Boleyn's maids of honour; and he describes one of these little bindings which is, unfortunately, lost.

FIG. 4.—*Le Chappellet de Ihesus, MS., sixteenth century.*
Margaret Tudor.

There is, however, one exquisite golden binding in existence which may be something like the books mentioned, only this one is recorded as having been given to the queen by one of the ladies of the Wyatt family. It is at present the property of Lord Romney, who is himself a descendant of that family, in whose possession it has always been since the sixteenth century. It is a Book of Prayers, and measures 2¼ inches in length, 1⅜ inch in breadth, and three-quarters of an inch in thickness. The designs upon it are most delicate and beautiful arabesques, very nearly resembling designs made by Hans Holbein for jewellery. These designs are left in low relief, the groundwork being cut away to a slight degree and filled with black enamel, so that the arabesques show in gold on a black ground. The back is panelled and decorated in the same way, as also are the clasps, of which there are two. There are rings at the two lower edges, for the suspension of the book at the girdle. It resembles much the little gold book described already as having belonged to Henry VIII., especially the back. It is figured and fully described in vol. xliv. of *Archæologia* at p. 260.

Another book which belonged to Anne Boleyn, and is said to have been with her on the scaffold, is in the British Museum. It is a copy of the New Testament in vellum, in English, printed at Antwerp in 1534 by Martin Emperowre. It has, unfortunately, been rebound for Mr. Cracherode, but still bears on its gilt and gauffred edges the words "*Anna Regina Angliæ*" written in red.

Henry VIII. made a most unjust will, confirmed nevertheless by Parliament and also acted up to by Edward VI., by virtue of which the succession to the throne of England was settled upon the descendants of his younger sister Mary, instead of those of his elder sister Margaret. The three grand-daughters of the Princess Mary were the Ladies Jane, Katherine, and Mary Grey. Lady Jane Grey, indeed, did come to the throne, as she was crowned Queen of England on the death of Edward VI., but she enjoyed the dignity but a short time, as nine days afterwards she was imprisoned in the Tower, and on February 12, 1554, was beheaded, aged only seventeen years. Her sisters both died prisoners. Edward VI., wishing to secure the Protestant succession, had named Lady Jane Grey as his successor, but the Roman Catholic influence was at the time strong enough to neutralise the king's wishes, and the party of the Princess Mary prevailed for the present, the succession eventually reverting to its proper channel, the line of the Princess Margaret, who married James IV., King of Scotland.

One volume alone remains that bears upon its binding evidence of having belonged to Margaret Tudor, and this is one of great beauty. It was presented to the British Museum in 1864 by the Earl of Home, and is a manuscript of prayers with miniatures of French work called *Le Chappellet de Ihesus et de la Vierge Marie* (Fig. 4). It belonged first to Anna, wife of Ferdinand, King of the Romans in the sixteenth century. It is bound in green velvet and has silver clasps and bosses, partly gilt. The clasps have the letters "I.H.S." upon them, gilded, and the attachments of the clasps to the volume have the letters ANNA on them, one letter on each, gilded. These were evidently made for the first owner of the book. Then when it became the property of Queen Margaret, she added her name, MARGVERITE, on the sides in a very pretty manner, each letter, in silver, forming the centre of a double or Tudor rose, gilded. The inner rose has its petals smooth, and the outer one has its petals roughened, as are also the little leaves between each petal.

FIG. 5.—*Il Petrarcha. Venetia, 1544. Queen Katharine Parr.*

Henry VIII.'s younger sister Mary married first Louis XII. of France, and afterwards Charles Brandon, Duke of Suffolk, and there is one binding in the British Museum, purchased in 1865, which belonged to her as Duchess of Suffolk. It is an Herbal printed at Frankfort in 1535, and is bound in dark calf, decorated with blind lines and gold stamped work. The broad outer border has at first sight the appearance of a roll stamp, but it is not actually so, the effect being produced by the successive impressions of a long rectangular stamp having engraved upon it a pattern which, on being repeated, gives the appearance of a continuous design. The design on this stamp is original and simple, and has no "Italian" origin at all. The inner panel has mitre-lines in blind at each of the angles, the points of junction with the outer border being covered with a fleur-de-lis, and then converging lines meet an inner rectangular line which encloses the royal coat-of-arms of England, crowned, the two upper corner-spaces being occupied by double roses, and the two lower by the portcullis badge and chains, all impressed in gold. At the sides of the inner panel are the initials "M. S.," presumably standing for "Mary Suffolk." The workmanship of this curious volume is coarse and irregular, but there is a boldness about it that is not without charm, and the design itself is well balanced and effective.

Queen Katharine Parr has the reputation of having herself worked the cover of a copy of Petrarch printed at Venice in 1544, and bound in purple velvet (Fig. 5). It is embroidered in coloured silks and gold and silver thread. The design is a large coat-of-arms, that of Katharine herself, with many quarterings, the first being the coat of augmentation granted to her by the king. The coat is surmounted by a royal crown, but the supporters are those of the families of Fitzhugh and Parr; so the work was probably done before Katharine was married to Lord Seymour, but after the king's death. The work is somewhat faded, and the scroll-work in gold cord at the corners is pulled out of place, no doubt the result of bad re-covering, but altogether it is in excellent condition, and is a fine specimen of royal workmanship. The Princess Elizabeth worked the cover of *The Miroir or Glasse of the Synneful Soul* for Queen Katharine. It is said to have been worked when the Princess was only eleven years old, and it is certainly possible as the workmanship is simple, indeed such as a clever girl might easily do. It is braid work of gold and silver on a blue silk ground. This ground is probably woven with a very large mesh, and is similar to that used by the Princess on the little Book of Prayers she worked for her father. The initials of the queen, "K. P.," occupy the place of honour in the centre, and are enclosed in an elaborate interlaced arrangement of lines and knots of braid, and in each corner, in high relief, is a heartsease, Elizabeth's favourite flower. The volume is now in the Bodleian Library at Oxford.

It is, moreover, an interesting proof of the learning of the Princess Elizabeth, as she says it was translated by herself "out of Frenche ryme into English prose, joyning the sentences together as well as the capacitie of my symple witte and small lerning coulde extende themselves," and it is charmingly dedicated "To our most noble and vertuous quene Katherin," to whom Elizabeth, "her humble daughter, wisheth perpetuall felicitie and everlasting joye."

CHAPTER II

EDWARD VI.—MARY AND ELIZABETH

There are specimens of books bound for Edward VI. in the British Museum, both before and after his accession to the throne. Most, if not all of these, in leather, are probably the work of Thomas Berthelet, as they have many points in common, and he continued the "King's printer servaunt," and furnished him also with bindings.

The earliest of these is a manuscript by Petrus Olivarius, *In Trogum Pompeium et in Epistolas familiares Ciceronis, Chorographica*, presented by the author to Prince Edward in 1546, and it bears in the centre the Prince of Wales' feathers within a flamed circle. A somewhat more elaborate binding, with the royal coat-of-arms of England within a flamed circle, occurs on another manuscript, a translation by William Thomas of a book of travels, which is also dedicated to the king. A similar design to this last book is found on the binding of *Xenophon, La Cyropédie*, printed in Paris in 1547. It is covered in rich brown calf, and each panel is ornamented with an interlacing fillet, coloured black, enclosing an inner diamond, in the centre of which is the royal coat-of-arms, with "E. R." and a double rose above and below. The spaces are filled with arabesques, cornucopiæ, and small stars. The colouring of the fillets, with black stain on calf, is a characteristic of Berthelet's work for Edward VI. and Mary. This peculiarity does not occur, as far as I know, on any of those he bound for Henry VIII., so it may be considered that the black fillets, often interlaced in a masterly way, and frequently arranged in semicircular forms, are evidence of the later work of this master of his art. At the same time, many of the smaller stamps used on these later volumes are found also on the earlier examples. But whereas in the earlier style so-called "Italian" designs are used, it appears to me that in his later and finer style Berthelet has given us a very noble series of books decorated in an original and strikingly effective manner. The contrast of the rich brown calf with the black of the fillets and the rich gold of the stamped lines and designs is often beautiful. The finest example of this style is to be found in the Museum copy of Cardinal Bembo's *Historia Veneta*, printed at Venice in 1551. It is a large book measuring 12 × 9 inches, and the single black fillet is most cleverly interlaced with corners, circles, and semicircles, in such a manner as, in fact, to form a triple border, in the centre of which is the royal coat-of-arms, itself surrounded by a line of curves finished at the ends with double roses and arabesques, and flanked at each side with the crowned initials of the king. In a circle at the upper part of the board is the motto "Dieu et mon droyt"; and in a corresponding circle at the lower part is the date "MDLII." The spaces throughout are filled with arabesques, cornucopiæ, double roses, and small stars. The back of the book is curiously arranged so as to look like the front, so that it appears to have no back at all.

Gualteri Deloeni Commentarius in tres prima Capitula Geneseos, etc., a manuscript dedicated to Edward VI., is bound in a very delightful and simple manner, and one which, for a small book, is nearly perfect in taste. It is covered in rich brown calf, and ornamented with blind lines and gold—a contrast which Berthelet uses, especially on small bindings. The "blind" work in these cases appears to be purposely darkened, which can easily be done by using the tools hot, or by the addition of a little printer's ink. In the centre of this binding is the royal coat-of-arms surmounted by a crowned double rose. This is flanked by two cornucopiæ; at the sides of the shield itself are the king's initials, "E. R.," and under each of them the daisy with stalk and leaves. The same cornucopia stamp is used at each of the four inner corners, and each of the four outer corners is ornamented with a conventional floral stamp.

King Edward VI. not only had his bindings stamped with his royal badges, but the edges also sometimes came in for a share of attention, as on a copy of *La Geografia di Claudio Ptolemeo*, printed at Venice in 1548. On the front or fore-edge of the book is the royal coat-of-arms of England, painted on a blue ground; on the upper edge is the coat-of-arms of France, and on the lower the golden harp of Ireland. The side space on each of these edges is filled up with a delicate arrangement of interlacing strap-work in black, and further ornamented with fine gold scrolls and the initials "E. S. R.," also in gold.

One of Edward's books, however, has actually the first instance in an English book of a decorated "doublure," the name by which we understand the inner side of the boards of a book.

Mr. Herbert Horne, in his most excellent work on the *Binding of Books*, mentions, and gives a plate of, an instance of this kind of decoration occurring on a copy of Petrarch, printed at Venice in 1532. It is an arrangement of interlaced lines of silver with two figured stamps, and is said to be the earliest European example. Edward VI.'s doublure (Fig. 6) is not much later, as it was probably bound about 1547, and, like nearly all doublures, it is in a wonderful state of preservation; in fact, it may be said to be the only instance of a sixteenth-century painted book that is at all in its original state, as the pigment used upon them is extremely delicate, and chips off freely. The book, a small duodecimo, is covered in crimson velvet, much worn, and is a collection of "certeine prayers and godly meditacyons," printed at Malborow in 1538. The inner side of each of the boards is covered with calf, and the design is outlined in gold and filled in with colour. This colour is not quite like oil-paint, but resembles closely the "enamel" colours which have of late years been so well known. It has little penetrating quality, lying evenly on the top of the leather, and dries with an even and polished surface. The king's arms, crowned, occupy the centre of the board, the arms in the correct heraldic colours and the crown of gold, silver, blue, and green. The king's initials, stamped in gold, are on each side of the shield. A rectangular border of green encloses the coat-of-arms, and at each of the inner corners is a daisy in gold, and above and below the arms is a semicircular projection from the green border, coloured blue.

FIG. 6.—*Prayers, etc. Malborow, 1538 (Doublure). Edward VI.*

There is yet another volume which for many years has been by the British Museum authorities attributed to Edward VI., but Mr. W. Y. Fletcher, in his splendid volume on the *English Bookbindings in the British Museum*, considers it to be Elizabethan. There is no doubt that the volume in some ways fits a description of one that was presented to that queen by the University of Oxford at Woodstock in 1575, but I think the difference in the dates of printing and presentation is a weak point in the argument. The book was printed in 1544 at Zurich, and it certainly seems curious that a book printed thirty-one years before should be offered as a present to a reigning sovereign.

So for the present I shall adhere to its former description in the show-case in the King's Library, and describe it here in its place as having been bound for Edward VI. It is covered in green velvet, with a border parallel to the sides stamped in gold and bearing the legends, "ESTO FIDELIS USQUE AD MORTEM ET DABO TIBI CORONAM VITÆ—APOC. 2" on one side, and on the other "FIDEM SERVAVI QVOD SVPEREST REPOSITA EST MIHI CORONA JVSTITIÆ—2 TIM. 4." In the centre of each cover is the royal coat-of-arms enclosed within a Garter, crowned, appliqué in pieces of coloured silk and stamped in gold, beautifully designed and beautifully executed, and the first instance of velvet or silk stamped in gold that is known to me. On the gilt edges designs are stamped, or "gauffred" as it is called, and painted. On the front edge the arms of the University of Oxford. On the upper edge a crowned Tudor rose with the initials E. R., and on the lower a portcullis with the same initials. There are other instances where the similarity between the emblems and initials of these two sovereigns, Edward VI. and Elizabeth, causes considerable doubt as to which of them was actually the owner, and I think that generally the date of the printing of such books must be considered as some authority, although among the arguments for or against the attribution of a binding to any particular owner, or author, it may be said that the date of the printing of the book must generally be esteemed at a small value.

A book which has some of the peculiarities of Berthelet's work upon it is found in a copy of Bude's *Commentarii Linguæ Græcæ*, printed at Paris in 1548. It is covered in calf, and has a rectangular border running parallel with the edges of the boards on each side. This border is coloured black, but it has the uncommon addition of stamped arabesques in gold upon this black. At the outer corners are arabesques in outline, and in the inner corners double roses stamped in gold. In the centre a framework of two interlaced squares, stained black, enclose the royal coat-of-arms and initials.

The same workman who executed this binding also made one for Queen Mary, which I shall describe further on.

At Windsor there is a fine little binding on a copy of *Strena Galteri Deloeni: ex capite Geneseos quarto deprompta*, etc. It is bound in white leather, and ornamented with the royal coat-of-arms in the centre, flanked by the letters "E. R.," and surrounded by a scattered arrangement of double roses, daisies, cornucopiæ, and stars, all enclosed in a small decorated border. It is probably by Berthelet, and is in excellent condition. In the British Museum there are instances of bindings in white leather made for Henry VIII. and for Mary, but there is no instance of one made for Edward VI., so that this Windsor binding is of considerable interest apart from its beauty.

A copy of Herodotus' and Thucydides' works, bound together in one cover, belonged most likely to Edward VI. It is part of the old royal library, and is bound in brown calf, with a broad outer border of Italian character enclosing the royal coat-of-arms, crowned, within a flamed circle. The flamed circle first occurs, as may have been noted, on the volumes bound for Edward when Prince of Wales, and it is afterwards used on several of his later volumes, and also on many that were bound for Queen Mary. What the meaning of this flamed circle is I have not been able to conjecture, it may possibly only be intended for ornament. Berthelet, doubtless, liked to use circles or parts of circles on his bindings, and in this taste he was following the lead of much more ancient English binders, as the circle is characteristic of the splendid blind stamped English work of the twelfth and thirteenth centuries.

Thomas Berthelet died, according to an entry in the Stationers' Company Register, in 1556. So that it is just possible he bound books for Queen Mary. But I think that Berthelet was quickly copied, and it is very easy to copy the style or even the actual stamps of any binder; and if the binding of Cardinal Bembo's *History of Venice* be taken as a test example of Berthelet's best work, which I think it fairly may be, it will be seen that although Mary's bindings have some points of resemblance there are also many wide differences. Berthelet avowedly acknowledged the beauty of Italian originals, but I do not find that he actually copied any one of them, and he, moreover, very soon left them behind. There is a certain recrudescence of this Italian manner distinctly apparent in many of the books bound for Queen Mary, and I imagine this to be the work, not of Berthelet himself, but of one of his imitators or successors, or perhaps one of his own workmen.

A good example of this Italian-English style is found on the binding of the *Epitome omnium operum Divi Aurelii Augusti*, etc., printed at Cologne in 1549. A very handsome broad border containing an elaborate arabesque is parallel to the edges of the boards. This encloses an inner black fillet interlaced with a diamond, in the middle of which is the royal coat-of-arms within a flamed circle, and at each side, in the angles formed by the intersection of the diamond points and the inner rectangular lines, are the initials M. R. The spaces throughout are filled in with arabesques, single roses, and circles.

A very similar design occurs on the binding of a manuscript poem by Myles Haggard, addressed to the queen, and another on a copy of Bonner's *Profitable Doctrine*, printed in London in 1555.

Entirely different in manner of decoration is the binding of the *Commentary on the New Testament*, in Latin, by Aurelius Augustinus, printed at Basle in 1542, and which came to the British Museum as part of the old royal library. It is covered in white leather, and ornamented with gold tooling of a very elaborate kind. A broad inner rectangular panel, broken outwards at each side, contains a diamond, and the spaces in and about these leading lines are filled with arabesques, royal arms, and royal emblems, roses, fleurs-de-lis, and portcullises. Although the general design of the original decoration of this book has doubtless been preserved, it has been grievously tampered with, and no reliance can be put on any of the small detail work now existing upon it—a most unlucky circumstance, as it is unlike any other royal book in the general arrangement of its ornamentation, and so of special interest.

So again different, but in a much less important manner, is the little calf binding of a *Livre faisant mention de sept parolles que N. S. Jesuchrist dit en l'arbre de la croix*, printed at Paris in 1545, and bound for Queen Mary. It is decorated with blind and gold lines, and dotted all about in the most reckless manner with M's and I's, meaning doubtless Mary the First. In the centre of each cover there is a knot, the same knot exactly as is used in the sculptures on our Houses of Parliament to tie together the initials V. R. of our present Most Gracious Queen, and surrounding the knot are four M's. The I's are down the edge of the boards nearest to the back. The little book is of great interest, as it never could have been in any way a State copy, but was most likely a favourite book of the queen's, and so decorated with her initials only—leaving heraldry for once out of the scheme.

The most splendid of the books that Queen Mary has left for us to admire is a manuscript of Psalms and Hymns in Latin and French of very beautiful workmanship, known as Queen Mary's Psalter. It came to the British Museum with the old royal library. It is bound in crimson velvet and has gilt clasps and corners, and on each side a large piece of embroidery appliqué. This embroidery is much worn; it is on canvas, and some of it is actually gone, but it seems to have been a conventional pomegranate, and this is all the more likely as such a design would have been a probable one for Queen Mary to use, as she had an excuse to do so by virtue of her mother's right to the emblem of Arragon. The clasps are engraved with the dragon, lion, portcullis, and fleur-de-lis, and in spite of the damage done to the volume by time and wear, it is still a splendid specimen of magnificent binding. By an inscription at the end of the volume we are informed that it was rescued from the hands of some seamen who were preparing to carry it abroad by "Baldwin Smith," who presented it to Queen Mary in 1553.

FIG. 7.—*Queen Mary's Psalter, MS.*

A book of hours in illuminated manuscript is beautifully bound for Queen Mary, and is finished in an unusually delicate manner. It is in calf, and has blind and gold lines. An outer border has stamps within it at intervals, in a similar style to one already described as having belonged to Edward VI. In the centre of the book is a delicate stamp of the royal coat-of-arms with the letters M. R.

At Stonyhurst College is preserved Queen Mary's own *Horæ in laudeum Beatissimæ Virginis Marie*, Lugduni, 1558. It is covered in figured red velvet projecting over the boards at the lower edges, and with small tassels at each corner. On the lower cover is the crowned coat-of-arms in silver, enamelled in the proper colours. Single ornamental letters R.E.G.I.N.A. are arranged in couples in three lines round it. On the upper board are the letters M.A.R.I.A., also in silver. The first two at the two top corners, the R crowned in the middle, and the two last letters in the two lower corners. The R in the centre is flanked by a double rose and the pomegranate of Arragon, both in silver. There are two silver clasps of ornamental pattern. It was shown at the Burlington Fine Arts Club Exhibition on Bookbindings in 1891, and there is a fine plate of it in their Illustrated Catalogue.

The bindings of Edward VI. and Mary, having as a chief ornament the English coat-of-arms, nevertheless bear with them no supporters. Henry VII. and Henry VIII., until 1528, used the same supporters, the dragon on the dexter side and the white greyhound on the sinister; and when Henry VIII. made a change and adopted the crowned lion as one of his supporters, he omitted the greyhound and changed the side of the dragon, so that his successors bore as their supporters a lion crowned on the dexter side and the red dragon on the sinister, and so they occur on several Elizabethan bindings.

FIG. 8.—*Prayers, etc. London, 1574-1591. Queen Elizabeth.*

The bindings executed for Queen Elizabeth may be conveniently divided into three classes—those bound in, or ornamented with, gold; those bound in velvet or embroidered; and those bound in leather. In this order I shall describe them. The gold, as far as I know it, is always enamelled, the velvet is generally embroidered, and the leather is frequently inlaid with other and differently coloured leathers. The peculiarity of sunken panels, borrowed apparently through the early Italian bindings from Oriental originals, is a remarkable speciality of Elizabethan work; as is also the first use of large corner-stamps to any extent. There certainly are instances of corner-stamps on Henry VIII. bindings, but they are rare; whereas with Elizabeth and her immediate successors the use of such stamps is very usual. The finest, as well as the most interesting, of the golden books made for Elizabeth is one containing prayers and devotional pieces by Lady Elizabeth Tyrwhitt, printed for Chris Barker, London, 1574. It also contains the queen's prayers, a collection out of other works, and part of an Almanack for 1583-91 (Fig. 8). In 1790 it belonged to the Rev. Mr. Ashley, and it was presented to the British Museum in 1894 by Sir Wollaston Franks. It measures 2¼ inches by 1¾. On each side is a sunken panel, round which is a flat border containing texts from Scripture, engraved and run in with black enamel. The upper cover of the book has a representation in gold of the serpent in the wilderness and the stricken Israelites. The serpent on the tree and others on the ground, and the figures of the people, are all carved in very high relief, and enamelled in colours; the flesh being represented by white. The serpents are in blue. Round this design are the words "MAKE · THE · AFYRYE · SERPENT · AN · SETIT · VP · FORA · SYGNE · THATAS · MANY · ASARE · BYTTE · MAYELOKE · VPONIT · AN · LYVE+." On the lower cover a similar panel contains a representation of the judgment of Solomon, worked in a similar way. Round this runs the legend, "THEN · THE · KYNG · ANSVERED · AN · SAYD · GYVE · HER · THE · LYVYNG · CHILD · AN · SLAYETNOT · FOR · SHEIS · THEMOTHER · THEROF—1 K. 3 C+." The back is divided into four panels, each of which has a delicate and graceful arabesque engraved and run in with black enamel, as also have the two clasps. There are two rings at the top, in order that the book might be worn at the girdle. There is no real record as to who worked this enamel, but it is credited to George Heriot, afterwards goldsmith and banker to James I., and founder of the George Heriot Hospital at Edinburgh. It is in very good condition, and but little of the enamel has chipped off. It is now preserved in the Gold Room at the British Museum. It is the only one of Elizabeth's golden books that is worked in high relief, and such work is undoubtedly of the greatest rarity.

For actual beauty of workmanship, it would be difficult to find any specimen of finer execution than that which occurs on the binding of a little volume of Christian meditations in Latin printed in 1570, and bound in rose-coloured velvet, with clasps, centre-pieces, and corners all bearing delicate champlevé enamel-work on gold (Fig. 9). The book is quite a small one, measuring 5 × 3¼ inches, and the workmanship on the gold is of corresponding delicacy. In the centre of each cover a thin diamond of gold is fixed, the outline being broken in each case by a series of small decorative curves. Each diamond is further ornamented with the Tudor rose, ensigned with the royal crown, and flanked by the initials E. R. The rose is red with small green leaves, the cup of the crown is blue, and the initials are in black enamel. The whole of the vandyked edge of the diamond is bordered with a thin line of blue enamel, and the remaining spaces are filled up with small floral sprays having green leaves and red and blue flowers. The corner-pieces are ornamented in a similar way with set patterns of arabesques and flowers in red, blue, green, and yellow enamels, as also are the clasps. These enamels are all what is called translucent, and many of the colours are remarkable for their brilliancy and beauty, as well as for the skill with which they are used. The engraving of the gold plate, which is filled by these enamels, is also of remarkable beauty. George Heriot again is credited with this work, with perhaps some show of probability.

FIG. 9.—*Christian Meditations, in Latin, 1570.*
Queen Elizabeth.

One more book in the British Museum has champlevé enamels upon it, evidently by the same workman. It is a New Testament in Greek printed at Paris in 1550. It is now bound in green velvet,—but this probably was the original material in which it was covered,—and in the centre of each of the boards is a diamond-shaped panel of gold, 2¾ inches in length and 2¼ in breadth (Plate II.) Judging from the analogy of the smaller book just described, there probably were originally corners and clasps to this book, but they are now gone. Each of the diamonds has originally borne rich-coloured enamels, but by far the greater part of this has chipped off, only small pieces remaining here and there in corners. On the upper cover the diamond contains the royal coat-of-arms of England, surrounded with floral sprays, roses, and flies. The diamond on the lower cover of the book has a red rose, crowned, contained in a circular border, the spaces within and without the circle being filled with similar sprays to those upon the other side. Among them are acorns and flies again. The delicate engraving on the gold of both these diamonds can be very well studied, as the marks of the engraving are easily apparent.

Paul Heutzner visited England in 1598, and examined the royal library at Whitehall. In his *Itinerarium* he says: "The books were all bound in velvet of different colours, chiefly red, with clasps of gold and silver, some having pearls and precious stones set in their bindings." It is rather curious he should have mentioned red, because, although there are many books in velvet that were bound for Queen Elizabeth, the only one I know of in red is the little volume described above, all the rest being in green, black, or purple. Dibdin, in his *Bibliomania*, says that Princess Elizabeth, when she was a prisoner at Woodstock in 1555, worked a cover of a little book which is now in the Bodleian Library at Oxford. It now contains a small copy of the Epistles of St. Paul printed by Barker in 1578, so that, if Dibdin is right in saying that Elizabeth worked it when she was at Woodstock, it cannot have been worked for the book it now covers. Certainly, the embroidered portion has been at some time or other relaid in its present position, and considerable damage has resulted from the operation. Inside is a note in Elizabeth's handwriting, in which she says: "I walke manie times into the pleasant fieldes of the Holye Scriptures, where I plucke up the goodlie green herbes of sentences by pruning, eate them by reading, chawe them by musing, and laie them up at length in the hie seat of memorie by gathering them together, so that having tasted thy swetenes, I may the less perceave the bitterness of this miserable life." The material is, or was, black velvet, but the pile is entirely gone, except in a few protected corners. The design is outlined in silver cord, and the raised portions are worked with silver guimp. An outer border, with lettering, encloses in each case a central design. The motto on the border of the upper cover reads, "CELUM PATRIA SCOPUS VITÆ X P V S. CHRISTUS VIA, CHRISTO VIVE." That round the lower cover, "BEATUS QUI DIVITIAS SCRIPTURÆ LEGENS VERBA VERTIT IN OPERA." Within the border, on the upper cover, is a ribbon arranged in a long oval bearing the words "ELEVA COR SURSUM IBI UBI E. C. (*i.e.* est Christus)." The E and the C are in larger type, and between them is a heart in raised work, through which passes a stem, the lower end of which has two small leaves and the top a flower. On the lower cover a similar ribbon bears the words "VICIT OMNIA PERTINAX VIRTUS E. C." These two last letters, Dibdin says, means "Elizabetha Captiva," in support of his theory that it was worked by her at Woodstock. In the centre of the oval on this lower cover is an eight-petalled flower with stem and two leaves. The record of this book is remarkably clear. But, besides this, there is little doubt, judging it by other work of Queen Elizabeth, that it was executed and probably designed by herself. All the books credited to her with any show of probability are worked in braid or thick cord, and the designs on each are of a simple character.

The most decorative of all the embroidered books worked for Queen Elizabeth is now, unfortunately, in the worst condition of any of them. It is a copy of Bishop Christopherson's *Historia Ecclesiastica*, Louvanii, 1569, divided into three volumes, each measuring about 6 inches by 3½. It is covered in green velvet, and each side is ornamented in the same way. In the centre a long oval shield, appliqué, in silks of the proper colour. The bearings, worked in gold thread, are enclosed in an oval of pink satin studded with a row of small pearls. Surrounding this is a decorative Elizabethan border worked in gold thread and pearls. The rest of the board is closely covered with a rich design of arabesques and roses in gold cord and guimp, the roses being "Tudor," with red silk centres and pearl outer petals, and "York," worked entirely with small seed pearls. The narrow outer border, formed by an interlacing ribbon outlined in gold cord, has an inner row of seed pearls along its entire length; and many of the spaces all over the side of the book have small single seed pearls in them. The back is divided into five panels, bearing alternately white and Tudor roses of the same kind of work as those on the sides of the book, only on a larger scale. There have also been many supplementary pearls on the back of the book. A large majority of the pearls are unfortunately now missing, as is also a great part of the gold cord, so that the above description is in fact a restoration. But every pearl and every piece of cord that is wanting has left a distinct impression on the velvet.

One of the most celebrated of all embroidered books done in England was executed for Queen Elizabeth. It is a large book measuring 10 inches by 7, and is an account by Matthew Parker, Archbishop of Canterbury, *De antiqvitate Britannicæ Ecclesiæ*, etc. It was privately printed by John Day at Lambeth Palace in 1572 for the Archbishop, being the first book of the kind issued in England. It is supposed to have been a presentation copy to the queen. It is covered in deep green velvet. On both covers the outer border is worked in gold, in a pattern resembling a wooden park paling, and it is probable that each side is meant to represent a park, thereby indicating the author's name of Parker. Within this paling on the upper cover is a design of a large rose-tree with Tudor roses, and Yorkist and Lancastrian roses, all growing upon it. Besides these flowers there are heartsease, daisies, carnations, and others whose species is difficult to determine. In the four corners of the "park" are four deer, their eyes being indicated with little black beads, some gambolling, some feeding, and on the groundwork are many grass-tufts of gold thread. The central design on the under cover is not by any means so fine. It has several plants scattered about it. There are two snakes brilliantly worked in gold and silver cord and coloured silks, and five deer like those on the other side. Originally there were red silk ribbons to tie the book together at the front edges, but there is only a trace of them now left. The back is divided into five panels, bearing alternately white and Tudor roses, with leaves, stems, and buds. It is said that Archbishop Parker kept in his own house "painters ... writers, and bookbinders," so it is very likely that this book was bound under his own eyes. It is said that only twenty copies of it were printed, and that no two were alike. It contains the biographies of sixty-nine Archbishops, but not Parker's own. This omission was afterwards supplied by the publication of a little satirical tract, in 1574, entitled *Histriola, a little Storye of the Actes and Life of Matthew, now Archbishop of Canterbury*. The two title-pages and the leaf with the Archbishops' coats-of-arms are vellum, and the woodcuts, borders, and arms throughout the volume are emblazoned in gold and colours. It is now part of the old royal collection in the British Museum.

FIG. 10.—*Parker. De antiqvitate Britannicæ Ecclesiæ. London, 1572. Queen Elizabeth.*

A small copy of the New Testament in Greek, printed at Leyden in 1576, is covered in white ribbed silk, and embroidered in gold, for Queen Elizabeth. Each board has the same pattern upon it; in the centre the royal arms of England, ensigned with the crown, and surrounded by the Garter, in both of which are inserted several seed pearls. This is surrounded by an irregular border of thick gold cord, interlaced, in which are leafy sprays of single and double roses. The arrangement of this border is admirably designed. The colours of the arms, the Garter, and the red roses are painted, probably in water-colours, on the silk itself—the earliest specimen of such work that is known to me. From the delicacy of the material on which the embroidery is done, and the high projection of many of the threads, the book has evidently got into very bad condition at a remote period; and it has been entrusted to some one to repair, who has removed all the original binding and re-inlaid it on new boards, the result being that he has increased the damage already existing.

A little book, *Orationis Dominicæ Explicatio, per Lambertum Danaeum*, printed at Geneva in 1583, is covered in black velvet, and ornamented with a very effective design, worked with broad gold cord (Fig. 11). An outer arabesque border, having also flowers of silver guimp, encloses an inner panel which has two white roses in the centre, and a red rose in each of the inner corners. Each of these roses has a little green leaf at the junction of the petals, and they are apparently outlined with silver thread. It is, however, often difficult with old books to say for certain whether a thread has been gold or silver, as the gold cord has a tendency to wear white, and the silver cord often turns yellow. The contrast of colour on this little book is very charming even now, and it must have been particularly beautiful when it was first done. It has the remains of ties at the front edges of red silk and gold cord.

There is another embroidered book belonging to the old royal collection in the British Museum that seems to have been bound for Queen Elizabeth. It is a copy of *The Common Places of Dr. Peter Martyr*, translated by Anthonie Marten, printed in London in 1583, and dedicated to the queen. It is covered in blue purple velvet, and ornamented with silver wire and guimp. There is an outer border formed of double lines, made easily and effectively by means of a spiral wire flattened down, giving the appearance of small overlaid rings. This border encloses a series of clusters, formed with stitches of silver guimp, arranged in a basket-work pattern. In the centre is an ornament of diamond shape, outlined with the same silver-wire edge and enclosing again the basket-work design, and the four inner corners are filled up with quarter circles of the same work. The book has been rebacked, and it is not in very good condition; but the effect of the silver on the deep purple ground still has a very admirable effect. The broad gilt edges are very handsomely and elaborately decorated with gauffred work of Elizabethan character.

A Bible, printed in London in 1583, was embroidered and bound for Queen Elizabeth, and presented to her in 1584, and is now in the Bodleian Library at Oxford. It is a folio book, measuring almost 17 × 12 inches, and is bound in crimson velvet. Upon each board is a very graceful design of rose-branches, intertwined. There are four large roses and two smaller ones, all embroidered in silver and gold braid and coloured threads, with here and there a few small pearls. A narrow border runs round the edge, embroidered in gold thread and coloured silk.

FIG. 11.—*Orationis Dominicæ Explicatio, per L. Danaeum. Genevae, 1583. Queen Elizabeth.*

A remarkable binding on calf, executed for Queen Elizabeth, is on a large Bible printed at Lyons, measuring 16½ inches by 11, each board being double (Fig. 12). The upper board is pierced in several places, showing underneath it a lower level covered with green calf, and decorated with small stars and arabesques. The upper boards on both sides of the book are elaborately stamped in gold and painted in enamel colours, and in each case an oval, painted panel occupies the centre. The upper cover of the book has in the central oval a charming sunk miniature portrait of Elizabeth as a young woman, dressed in jewelled robes and head-dress, and carrying a sword or sceptre. The portrait is enclosed in a very delicately painted frame of jewelled goldsmith's work. This painting is unfortunately damaged, especially in the face, and it seems to be executed in opaque water-colours, varnished, on vellum. Immediately round the miniature, on the leather, is a very elaborately painted and gilded oval ribbon with the words "ELIZABETH DEI GRATIA ANG. FRAN. HIB. REGINA." The broad, irregular, oval border itself has a design of interlacing fillets and floral emblems of considerable beauty, winged horses and Cupids, all picked out in colours. This very large stamp, measuring 9 inches in length, which is now and then found on books other than royal, is the largest English stamp known to me. There are cartouches left in the upper leather above and below this central arrangement, and they are of a similar ornamentation and colour, as are also the very handsome corners. The other side of the book is similarly decorated, with the differences that the centre painting, by the same hand, is the royal coat-of-arms of England in an egg-shaped, oval form, surrounded by the Garter, within an Elizabethan scroll. Over the crown is a canopy of green and red, and the supporters of the lion and red dragon are in their proper places. Underneath the coat is the motto "DIEU ET MON DROIT" on an ornamental panel, and the legend lettered on the leather immediately surrounding the painting reads "POSUI DEUM ADIVTOREM MEUM." On the lower cartouche on this side is the date of the binding, "MDLXVIII." This binding, when new, must have been one of the finest and most elaborately decorated of any of the leather bindings made for an English sovereign. The back of the volume, nearly 5 inches in width, is also very finely ornamented with an Elizabethan pattern outlined in gold and coloured in keeping with the rest of the ornamental work. Its present condition is unfortunate. The restorations, which have been largely added, have, however, the merit of being at once apparent, as little or no trouble has been in this case taken to reproduce the old stamps. The gilt edges are beautifully gauffred, and are picked out here and there with colour. The design is a complicated arabesque with masks, and on the lower edge a curious design of an animal resembling a unicorn.

FIG. 12.—*La Saincte Bible. Lyon, 1566.*
Queen Elizabeth.

One more beautiful book in the old royal collection that belonged to Elizabeth has double boards. The outer edges on this instance are interesting, as there is, in fact, an elongated head-band running along their entire length and joining the edges of the two boards. It is covered in very dark morocco, and decorated in blind and gold stamped work. In the centre of each cover is a sunk oval medallion, on which is painted the royal coat-of-arms of England, surrounded by the Garter; the two supporters holding up the crown in their paws. Flanking the crown are the letters E. R. The motto "DIEU ET MON DROIT" is on a red panel with a blue border at the lower portion of the oval, and the groundwork of the whole is silver. The medallion is enclosed in a richly designed broad border of strap-work, enriched with dots and arabesques, all in gold. Towards the upper and lower corners are four silver double roses with gold crowns. In each corner is a quarter circle of vellum, pierced and richly gilded in a pattern of strap-work and floral sprays. All the foregoing is enclosed in a border of blind work, and an outer edging ornamented with a succession of small set stamps. There are traces of green ribbons, both on the front edges of the book and at the upper and lower edges. It is a copy of *Les Qvatre Premiers Livres des Navigations et Peregrinations Orientales de N. De Nicolay,* printed at Lyons in 1568, and probably bound at the same time. The book is especially remarkable for its vellum corners, which are actually inlaid; that is to say, a corresponding piece of morocco is cut out and replaced by the vellum. This process, which, of course, adds immensely to the power of a binder in decorating the outside of a book, is one which, so far as I am aware, does not occur before on any English binding. It is a fashion that was much followed in the next century both by French and English binders. In the great majority of instances, however, the added leather is not actually inlaid, but only scraped or cut very thin, and superimposed. The remarkable manner in which the two last books described are made up with double boards is worthy of special notice, and has not, I think, ever been used since on any sumptuous binding. The fashion is one, nevertheless, which was much used with great effect on fine Italian bindings made towards the end of the fifteenth century, and there are two books of this kind that belonged to Elizabeth, and were bound for her in Italy after the "Italian fashion," now in the British Museum. Vellum inlays for Queen Elizabeth occur in their finest form on a presentation copy from Matthew Parker, Archbishop of Canterbury, of *Hores Historiarvm, per Matthævm Westmonasteriensem Collecti,* etc., printed in London in 1570. It is probable that this volume was bound in Archbishop Parker's own house. It is covered in calf, and the centre, border, angles, and side-pieces are inlaid in white vellum, and richly stamped in gold. The actual centre of the boards has the royal coat-of-arms of England, with crown and Garter stamped in gold, enclosed in a vellum oval of strap-work and arabesques, with the letters E. R. at the sides. The inner parallelogram has large corners stamped in gold, and is edged with a black fillet, the entire field on the calf being decorated with a semée of triple dots. The book has two gilded clasps, and the edges of the leaves are gilt, gauffred, and painted. A small panel on each of the angle-pieces, which are otherwise ornamented with designs of military trophies, drums, trumpets, shields, swords, and cuirasses, bears the initials "J. D. P." These letters are supposed to mean John Day, Printer. John Day printed books at Lambeth for Archbishop Parker; and these corner-pieces do occur on books printed by him and bound in a very similar way to the volume now described, so there is some show of probability in the interpretation. A field covered with a succession of impressions from the same stamp has no name in English, but in France it is known as a "semée," its use having come into fashion in that country a little earlier than the date of this book.

FIG. 13.—*Gospels in Anglo-Saxon and English.*
London, 1571. Queen Elizabeth.

A smaller example, with centre-piece and angle inlays only, in all other ways exactly resembling the book just described, was printed in London, 1571 (Fig. 13). It is a copy of the Gospels printed by John Day, and is the dedication copy, as is stated in a MS. note on the title-page—"Presented to the Queen's own hands by Mr. Fox."

A copy, printed in London in 1575, of Grant's *Græcæ Linguæ Spicilegium* is covered in brown calf, and was bound for the queen. It has large corners stamped in gold from set stamps. In the centre it bears a fine stamp of the royal coat-of-arms, crowned, and surrounded by the Garter, and decorated with Elizabethan scrolls. The remainder of the groundwork is covered with a semée of small roses. Among the old royal manuscripts is a curious book, *Scholarum Etonensis ovatio de adventu Reginæ Elizabethæ*, 1563, covered in white vellum and stamped in gold. It bears in the centre the royal coat-of-arms enclosed in an oval ornamented border, and has large corner-pieces impressed from a set stamp, the field having a semée of small stars. The work upon this binding is of a curiously unfinished character, and it is probably the work of some unskilled local workman. The gilt edges are gauffred in a floral design, with some white colour here and there.

Anne Boleyn bore, as one of her many devices, a very decorative one of a crowned falcon holding a sceptre, standing on a pedestal, out of which is growing a rose-bush bearing white and red blossoms (Fig. 14). This badge occurs first in an illuminated initial letter to her patent of the Marquisate of Pembroke, and at her coronation, in a pageant at Whitehall, an image of the falcon played a prominent part. The origin of it is not very clear, but it may have been derived from the crest of Ormond, a white falcon, which is placed under the head of the Earl of Wiltshire, Queen Anne's father, on his tomb. It was in turn adopted by Queen Elizabeth, and was exhibited on the occasion of her visit to Norwich, in 1578, as her own badge; and it occurs also on the iron railing on her tomb in Henry VII.'s chapel. The queen bore it on several of her simpler bindings impressed in the centre of each board, with usually a small acorn spray at each corner. There are several books ornamented like this in the library of Westminster Abbey, and there are examples at Windsor. The British Museum possesses few, the best example being a copy of Justinus' *Trogi Pompeii Historiarum Philippicarum epitoma*, etc., printed at Paris in 1581. It originally had two ties at the front edge. At Windsor a few bindings of Elizabeth's are still preserved; among them, a copy of Paynell's *Conspiracie of Catiline* is bound in white leather, and bears the royal arms within a decorative border. It has large corners impressed by a set stamp, and has a semée of small flowers. A copy of Spenser's *Faerie Queene*, printed in London in 1590, also in the Windsor Library, bears in the centre a crowned double rose, in the centre of which is a portcullis, and E. B. at each side of it. The crowned rose was a favourite design with Elizabethan bookbinders; but unless there be corroborative evidence of royal possession, I do not think that the existence of this stamp is of itself a sufficient proof of such exalted ownership.

Mr. Andrew Tuer, in his admirable *History of the Horn-Book*, gives a figure of one which was exhibited in the Tudor Exhibition in 1890, where it was described as the *Horn-Book of Queen Elizabeth*. It is said to have been given by the queen to Lord Chancellor Egerton of Tatton, and it has been preserved in his family ever since. The letterpress is covered with a sheet of talc, and the back and handle are ornamented with graceful silver filigree work, that on the back being underlaid with red silk. Mr. Tuer thinks that the type used on this *Horn-Book* resembles some used by John Day, the printer already mentioned; and if so, it is not altogether unlikely that Archbishop Parker himself may have presented this beautiful toy to the queen, as well as the more serious works in velvet and inlaid leather.

FIG. 14.—*Centre stamp from Trogi Pompeii
Historiarum Philippicarum epitoma.
Parisiis, 1581.*

Although Mary Queen of Scots was not directly one of the sovereigns of
England, yet she is so intimately connected with them, both by her ancestry,
her own history, and her descendants, that the few bindings remaining that
belonged to her may well be included among these I am now describing. The
bindings that were done for her when she was Dauphiness, or Queen, of
France, are, like the Scottish ones, of great rarity. These French bindings are
always bound in black, and very often have black edges; and the only two
bindings known to me that belonged to her when Queen of Scotland are in
such dark calf that it is almost black also. The first and finest of these volumes
is a copy of the *Black Acts*, printed at Edinburgh, 1576. It is called *Black Acts*
from the character of the type, and is a collection of the Acts and
Constitutions of Scotland in force during the reigns of the Jameses and Mary
herself. The outer border on each side of the book is impressed in gold, and
consists of a broad arabesque design. Within this border is a representation
of the full coat-of-arms of Scotland—a lion rampant, within a treasure flory
counter-flory. The treasure should be double, but in this instance it is single.
The lion and the treasure are coloured red. Dependent from the shield is the
collar and badge of the Order of St. Andrew. A royal helmet, crowned, is
placed above the shield, and has a handsome mantling, coloured yellow. On

the crown is the crest of Scotland—a crowned lion sejant, holding in one paw a sceptre and in the other a sword. The lion is coloured red. The ancient supporters of Scotland, two white unicorns, are at each side of the shield; each bears a collar shaped like a coronet, with a long chain. Two standards are supported behind the shield; one bears the coat-of-arms of Scotland, and the other St. Andrew's Cross, both being in their proper colours. Across the top of these standards is a white scroll bearing the words "IN DEFENSE," and on similar scrolls just above the heads of the unicorns are the words "MARIA REGINA." There are a few thistles in outline scattered about. The workmanship of this piece of decoration is unlike that on any other book I know. It is what is called all "made up" by a series of impressions from small stamps, curves, and lines, and in places it seems to be done by hand by means of some sort of style drawn along on the leather, the mark being afterwards gilded. The appearance, indeed, is that of a drawing in gold-outline on the leather. The colour, which is freely used, is some sort of enamel, most of which has now chipped off, but enough of it is left to show what it has been originally. The book came to the Museum by gift from George IV. The edges are gauffred, with a little colour upon them.

The other book that belonged to Mary Queen of Scots was, in 1882, in the library of Sir James Gibson Craig. It is a folio copy of Paradin's *Chronique de Savoye*, printed at Lyons in 1552, and in Edinburgh Castle there is a list of treasures belonging to James VI., and "his hienes deerest moder," dated 1578, in which this book is mentioned. It is bound in dark calf, decorated in blind and gold. Each board has a broad border in blind nearly resembling that on the *Black Acts*. In the centre of each side is the royal coat-of-arms of Scotland in gold, crowned. Above, below, and on each side of it is a crowned "M." The crowned "M" is also impressed in gold at the outer corners of each board, and it is also in each of the seven panels of the back.

ΒΑΣΙΛΙΚΟΝ ΔΩΡΟΝ. M.S. Written for Prince Henry,
by King James VI. of Scotland.

James VI. of Scotland, whatever may have been his faults, certainly had the merit of knowing how to advise his son. In 1559 he wrote the curious *Basilicon Doron* for his "Dearest son Henry, the Prince." He writes as for a Prince of Scotland, and about the Scottish people, and when it was first issued there were many doubts as to its authorship. The original manuscript of this work is now part of the old royal library in the British Museum; and although a study of this most interesting manuscript will amply repay anybody who cares to read it, it is as well specially interesting because of the beautiful binding with which it is covered (Plate IV.) We know from documents that in 1580 John Gibson had been appointed binder to the King of Scotland, and that when he came to London this office was granted to John and Abraham Bateman; and, although no binding is certainly known to have been executed by either of these, I think it very probable that the binding of the *Basilicon Doron* may, for the present at all events, be attributed to John Gibson. It is covered in deep purple velvet, and the ornaments upon it are cut out in thin gold, and finished with engraved work. The design on each board is the royal coat-of-arms of Scotland, with supporters, crowned, and enclosed within the collar of the Order of the Thistle, dependent from which is the badge with St. Andrew. The supporters are the two unicorns standing upon a ribbon, on which is the legend, "IN MY DEFENSE. GOD ME DEFEND." Above the crown are two large letters, J. R. The corners and two clasps of the book are made in the form of thistles, with leaves and scrolls. Unluckily much of this gold work is gone, but in the figure I have restored it where necessary. The decoration altogether has a most rich and beautiful effect, and I know of no other book decorated in the same way. Indeed, books of any sort bound for James when he was king of Scotland are of the greatest rarity, and it is quite possible that this is the only existing specimen; although when he came to England a very large quantity of books were bound for him, the majority of which still remain.

CHAPTER III

JAMES I.—HENRY PRINCE OF WALES—CHARLES I.—CHARLES
II.—JAMES II.—WILLIAM AND MARY—ANNE

Up to the present, as far as bookbinding is concerned, I have only recorded one change in the royal coat of England, when Henry VIII., in 1528, altered his supporters, but on the accession of James I. to the throne of England a much greater and more important change took place. Not only was the shield of Scotland added, but also that of Ireland, which, although Elizabeth seems to have used it sometimes, was never before officially adopted. The harp of "Apollo Grian" has, equally with the Scottish coat, remained an integral part of our royal shield ever since. The coats of France and England were now quartered and placed in the first and fourth quarters, the coat of Scotland in the second quarter, and the coat of Ireland in the third. With minor changes and additions, this coat remained the same until the reign of George III., who, in 1801, finally omitted the coat of France. As to the supporters, James I. retained the crowned lion of Henry VIII., and substituted one of his white unicorns for the red dragon of Cadwallader; and these supporters remain unaltered to the present day.

The fashion of stamping in gold on velvet, one example of which I have already described as having been done for Edward VI. or Elizabeth, was practised to a considerable extent for James I., and there are several examples of it. James evidently thought much of the Tudor descent, by virtue of which he held his English throne; and he used the Tudor emblems freely. One large stamp was cut for him with the coat-of-arms just described within a crowned Garter, all enclosed in an ornamental oval border, in which are included the falcon badge of Queen Elizabeth, the double rose, portcullis, and fleur-de-lis of the Tudors, and the plume of the Prince of Wales. This stamp commonly occurs on leather bindings, but it also occurs, used with great effect, stamped in gold or velvet. A very charming specimen of this is on a copy of *Bogusz*, ΔΙΑΣΚΕΨΙΣ *Metaphysica*, printed on satin at Sedan, 1605, which is bound in crimson velvet, and has two blue silk ties at the front edge. At each of the four corners of the large stamp are four small decorative stamps. It is a presentation copy to James I., and has an autograph of Henry Prince of Wales inside the cover. In the Manuscript Department of the British Museum, belonging also to the old royal library, is a small book bound in dark green velvet, in the centre of which is stamped, in gold, the royal coat-of-arms within an ornamental border, into which is introduced the design of a thistle. An outer border of gold lines has decorative stamps at each corner. The manuscript is about the introduction of Christianity into England. These two designs, or amplifications of them, are the only ones that I have met with on stamped velvet bindings done for James.

There are a considerable number of books still remaining that belonged to James, bearing the royal coat-of-arms with supporters and initials, bound in leather. They often bear upon them rich semées, which form of ornamentation was used for James I. more than for any other sovereign. The semées generally consist of small lions passant, thistles, tridents, fleurs-de-lis, stars, or flowers. Books of this kind, with heavy corner-pieces, are so widely known that detailed description of them is hardly necessary; but there are modifications, some of which render the bindings of greater interest. One of these is a calf binding on *Ortelius, Theatrum Orbis Terrarum*, printed in London in 1606 (Plate V.) It measures 23 inches by 14, and when in its original state, was doubtless one of the finest bindings done for James I. The full coat-of-arms, with small inlays of red leather, is further coloured by hand, and is enclosed within a rectangular border. Between this and the corner-pieces is a very elaborate and graceful design of twining stems, leaves, and arabesques. The binding has been largely repaired, but the new stamps have been accurately copied from the old ones; and, except the outer border which is new, the design upon it is probably in all material points the same as it was originally.

Another instance of a departure from King James's stereotyped pattern occurs on Thevet's *Vies des hommes illustres*, printed at Paris, 1584. The crowned coat-of-arms in the centre, with the initials J. R., have inlays of red leather in the proper places, and the remainder of the board is so closely and intricately, with an ornamental design of dotted strap-work, interlaced with arabesques that no description can give much idea of it. The volume measures $15\frac{1}{2} \times 10\frac{1}{2}$ inches, and it is in perfect condition. Some doubt has been thrown upon the nationality of this most beautiful work, but Mr. Fletcher, in his splendid volume of *English Bookbindings in the British Museum*, has included it in his list. So perhaps in the future we may claim it as our own. There is one little point about it which, I think, may be considered as a reason for thinking it English work, and that is that the lions on the English coats are full face. On all the French bindings I know that were done for English sovereigns the lions are always shown side face.

A volume in the Manuscript Department of the British Museum, containing English and Italian songs with music, is bound in dark blue morocco, with unusually good corners, and the field adorned with large and beautiful stars. Large stars used in the field also occur on a vellum binding of the Abbot of Salisbury's *De Gratia et perve verantia Sanctorum*, printed in London, 1618. It is without the usual corner-stamps, and is in a most wonderful brilliant condition.

A little volume of King James's *Meditations on the Lord's Prayer*, London, 1619, is covered in deep purple velvet, with silver centre-piece, corners, and clasps. On the corners are engraved designs of the cross patée, thistle, harp, and fleurs-de-lis, all crowned. The corner with the crowned harp is, I believe, the first instance of this badge occurring on a book. The clasps are in the form of portcullises. The centre oval medallion has the royal coat-of-arms, Garter, and crown engraved upon it.

At the Burlington Fine Arts Club a fine specimen of binding for King James I. was exhibited by Mr. James Toovey. It is bound in white vellum, stamped in gold. In the centre are the royal arms, and it has large corner-stamps of unusual design, containing a sun with rays and an eagle, the ground being thickly covered with a semée of ermine spots. The border seems to be imitated from one of the old rolls of sporting subjects, which are mostly found on blind-tooled books at a much earlier period. It has squirrels, birds, snails, dogs, and insects. At Windsor there are a good many specimens of Jacobean bindings, all of them similar in character to one or other of the British Museum specimens that I have described at length.

Ortelius. Theatre of the World. London, 1606. James I.

Anne of Denmark, the queen of James I., does not appear to have possessed many books. There are only two in the British Museum that belonged to her, both of which are bound in vellum. The larger of the two, *Tansillo, Le Lagrime di San Pietro*, Vinegia, 1606, has a gold-line border with small floral corners, and in the centre the queen's paternal arms with many quarterings, the most important of which are Denmark, Norway, and Sweden. The coat is crowned, and above it are the letters "A. R."; and the queen's own motto, "La mia grandezza viene dal eccelso," is contained on a ribbon half enclosing the coat.

Prince Henry, the eldest son of James I., showed more taste for literary matters than any of his predecessors, although he was much addicted to all manly exercises. He not only took great interest in the books he already found in his father's library, but he materially added to it by further collections of his own. In 1609 he purchased the library of Lord Lumley, who had been his tutor, and which was the finest then in England, except that of Sir Robert Cotton. This library had originally belonged to Henry Fitz-Alan, Earl of Arundel, Lord Lumley's father-in-law, and it had been largely increased since his death. Prince Henry only possessed the library for three years, as he died in 1612, but during this time he made many important additions to it. Not many of the original bindings remain upon the Earl of Arundel's books, and those that do are usually simple. There is one specimen in the British Museum that is especially good; it bears a "cameo" of a white horse, galloping, with an oak spray in his mouth, in an oval medallion, and if there were many others like it, Prince Henry destroyed much beautiful work when he had them rebound.

It must be supposed that the bindings of both Lord Arundel's and Lord Lumley's collection were in a bad state when Prince Henry acquired them, as they now are almost invariably in bindings that were made for him after 1610, when he was made Prince of Wales. On the Prince's death, his library, which was then kept at St. James's, reverted to the king, and served largely to augment the old royal library, which had not been very carefully kept up to the present time, and which, even afterwards, suffered various losses.

The majority of Prince Henry's rebindings are designed in a fashion which has been very adversely criticised, but nevertheless they are not all without interest. The commonest decoration found upon them consists of a large royal coat-of-arms of England within a scroll border with thistles, stamped in gold, having the label of the eldest son in silver. At the corners are very large stamps, either crowned double roses, fleurs-de-lis, lions rampant, all in gold, or the Prince of Wales' feathers in silver. Books bearing this design are more frequently met with outside the large royal collections than any others, as at one time or another many examples have become separated from the rest. But there are other books bound for the Prince the designs on which are often original and effective. Perhaps the best of these is on a copy of Livy's *Romana Historia*, Avreliæ Allobrogvm, 1609 (Fig. 15). In this instance the Prince of Wales' feathers form the central design, impressed in silver and gold, and with the initials H. P. at the sides of it, all enclosed in a border composed of a dotted ribbon arranged in right angles and segments of circles, enriched at the corners with ornamental arabesques. This design is particularly pleasing, and it is likely that it was executed by the same binder who bound the edition of Thevet's *Vies des hommes illustres*, described above, for James I., the peculiar design of the dotted ribbon appearing in both instances.

Petrus de Crescentiis, De omnibus agriculturæ partibus, Basileæ, 1548, has the Prince of Wales' feathers in silver, with H. P. at the sides, and on two upright labels the words "O et presidium | Dulce decus meum." It has very heavy corner-stamps.

A little book of *Commentaries* of Messer. Blaise de Monluc, Bordeaux, 1592, has a small Prince of Wales' feathers in the centre, and very pretty angle-stamps of sprays of foliage, the feathers still being in silver. *Rivault, Les Clemens d'Artillery*, Paris, 1608, is remarkably pretty. It is a small book bound in olive morocco, and has a tiny Prince of Wales' feathers in an oval in the centre, stamped in gold and silver, within a broad border of sprays of foliage. There are large angle-pieces of the same sprays, all enclosed in a border stamped in gold. A common design is the coat-of-arms, with label within an ornamental border, ensigned with a prince's crown, enclosed in a single line rectangle, at the corners of which are small stamps of the Prince of Wales' feathers, crowned roses, crowned fleurs-de-lis, and crowned thistles. There are several examples of this design, both in the British Museum and at Windsor.

FIG. 15.—*Livius. Romana Historia.*
Avreliæ Allobrogvm, 1609. Henry, Prince of Wales.

Pandulphi Collenucii Pisaurensis Apologus cui titulus Agenoria and other tracts in one collection was dedicated to Henry VIII., and originally his property (Fig. 16). It afterwards belonged to Magdalen College, Oxford, and they presented it to Prince Henry, for whom it was enclosed in a magnificent cover of crimson velvet, thickly embroidered with an elaborate design in gold and pearls. The edges of the cover project freely beyond the boards of the book, and have a rich gold fringe. The Prince of Wales' feathers, thickly worked in pearls, forms the centre of the design. The coronet is of gold, and the motto is in gold letters on a blue silk ground. The very beautiful broad border contains a rich arabesque design with flowers thickly worked in seed pearls, and the inner angles have sprays in gold and pearls. There are innumerable single pearls dotted about. Both for beauty of design and richness of execution, this cover is certainly one of the finest specimens of late embroidery work in England. With the exception of a few pearls missing, and some gold braid about the motto, it may be considered to be in a very fair condition.

Another crimson velvet book, *Becano Baculus Salcolbrigiensis*, Oppenheim, 1611, was bound for Prince Henry. It has the Prince of Wales' feathers in the centre, impressed in gold and silver, with a simple gold line round the edge. It is much faded, and the velvet is now more orange than crimson, but it is interesting as being the only instance in the British Museum of a stamped velvet book done for Prince Henry.

Prince Charles used two of the stamps which were first used by his brother Henry—the large coat-of-arms, with silver label, and the Prince of Wales' feathers. Each of these is usually flanked by the letters C. P., and the Prince of Wales' feathers are always stamped in gold instead of silver. In cases where Charles has used the coat-of-arms, the corners are filled with a full arrangement of leaf sprays and arabesques. A fine example of this style, bound in olive morocco, occurs on a binding of Dallington's *Aphorismes, Civill and Militarie*, London, 1613, now in the British Museum. An example of the Prince of Wales' feathers used alone on dark blue morocco is in the library at Windsor. During the reign of Charles I. several small, thin books were bound in vellum, stamped in gold (Plate VII.). Some of them were done for him both as prince and as king. A very good example covers a collection of Almanacks, dated 1624. In the centre is an ornament composed of four Prince of Wales' feathers arranged as a star, the corners are filled with large stamps, the remainder of the boards are filled with semées of flaming hearts. This particular book was probably a favourite one of the Prince's, as it contains his signature and other writings.

FIG. 16.—*Collection of Miscellaneous Tracts in MS.*
Henry Prince of Wales.

The styles of ornamentation used on large books for James I. were generally followed by his son, but often the outer borders are of a broader and more decorative kind. An instance of this is found on the dark morocco binding of Raderus's *Theological Biography*, printed at Munich in 1628, a large book with a broad decorative border, corner-pieces, coat-of-arms, and semée of thistles, roses, and fleurs-de-lis. A small book with coat-of-arms in the centre, within the Garter, crowned, and bearing on each cover the legend "TIBI SOLI O REX CHARISSIME," is in the Manuscript Department of the British Museum, on a collection of treatises presented to the king. There is a handsome border round the book, the ground of which is covered with a semée of crosses, and the letters C. R. are on either side of the coat-of-arms. The book has two silver clasps, on one of which is engraved the Scottish crest, and on the other three crowns. The panels joining the clasps to the book are engraved with emblematic figures.

A copy of *Hippocratis et Galeni opera*, Paris, 1639, in several volumes, bears in the centre of each board the full royal coat-of-arms and supporters, enclosed in an octagonal border, within a rectangle, in the inner corners of which is a handsome stamp of floral sprays, and at the outer corners the crowned monogram of King Charles and his wife Henrietta Maria. They are large books, measuring 17 × 11 inches.

A very decorative little book is covered in red velvet, with silver mounts. It is a copy of the New Testament, printed in London, 1643. On each side, in the centre, are medallion portraits of the king and his queen, in pierced and repoussé silver, within ornamental borders. On the panels of the clasps are engraved figures emblematic of the elements, and on the corner clasps emblematic figures of Charity, Justice, Hope, Fortitude, Prudence, Patience, Faith, and Temperance.

Although embroidered books were largely produced during the reign of Charles I., not many of them were made for himself. One exists in the British Museum, on a manuscript of Montenay's *Emblemes Chrestiens*, which is written by Esther Inglis, who was a calligraphist of great repute from the time of Queen Elizabeth to that of Prince Charles. She is said to have been nurse to Prince Henry; and it is probable that she worked the binding of the manuscript. It is covered in crimson satin, and embroidered in gold and silver cord with a few pearls. In the centre is the Prince of Wales' feathers enclosed in a laurel wreath, and round it a very handsome border, with arabesques at the inner corners.

New Testament, etc. London, 1643. Charles I.

A copy of the Psalms, printed in London in 1643, is covered in white satin and embroidered. It may have belonged to King Charles, and was purchased by the British Museum in 1888. In the centre, in an oval medallion, is a minute portrait of the king, wearing a crown with miniver cape and red robe, with the jewel of the Garter flanked by the letters C. R. Enclosing this is an arrangement of arabesques and flowers, worked respectively in silver or gold guimp and coloured silks. There is no record with the book, but it is quite possible that it was worked for the king. It is one of the smallest embroidered books existing, measuring little more than 3 inches by 2.

At Windsor there is a copy of the Book of Common Prayer, printed in 1638. It is bound in blue velvet, and richly embroidered in silver guimp. In the centre are the Prince of Wales' feathers, enclosed within a circular Garter, and surmounted by a prince's coronet, with C. P. on either side of it. Below are the rose and the thistle. A rich outer border of arabesques encloses the central design. Her Majesty lent this book to the Burlington Fine Arts Club in 1891. It was figured in the *Queen* of August 15, in the same year. There are several other bindings at Windsor that belonged to Charles; among them a particularly charming specimen covers a copy of *Ecphrasis Paraphraseos, G. Buchanani in Psalmos*, 1620. It is a small book, and bears the Prince of Wales' feathers in the centre, within a border of crosses, patée, and fleurs-de-lis, surrounded by the Garter. It has large corner-stamps and a semée of fleurs-de-lis. The other bindings made for Charles I. in the same library generally bear the royal coat-of-arms and large corner-stamps, and dates often occur upon them.

FIG. 17.—*Dallington. Aphorismes, Civill and Militarie. London, 1613. Charles Prince of Wales.*

Charles himself certainly took very considerable interest in bookbinding, and abundant evidence of this is found in the history of Nicholas Ferrar's establishment at Little Gidding, in Huntingdonshire, the beginning and ending of which was synchronous with Charles's reign. The king visited Little Gidding more than once, and always evinced the liveliest interest in its work, a very important part of which was bookbinding. The most remarkable feature about these Little Gidding bindings, which were the work of amateur hands, was the stamped work on velvet, which actually reached its highest development under the auspices, and probably by the hands, of some of the Collet family, nieces of Nicholas Ferrar. They bound books for Charles and for both his sons; but, unfortunately, no specimen of their finer stamped work done for either of these princes is in the British Museum.

The copy of the *Harmony of the Four Gospels*, known as "ΜΟΝΟΤΕΣΣΑΡΟΝ," which was given to Charles when Prince of Wales in 1640, is now in the library of the Earl of Normanton. It measures 24½ × 16 inches, and is bound in green velvet, stamped elaborately in gold. A *Concordance of the Four Evangelists*, which was probably made for James, Duke of York, about 1640, is now the property of the Marquis of Salisbury, and is kept at Hatfield. It measures 20 × 14 inches, and is bound in purple velvet. Among the small stamps upon it is one of a fleur-de-lis.

Gil. ΠΑΡΕΡΓΑ, etc. Londini, 1632. Charles I.

The Whole Law of God, as it is delivered in the Five Books of Moses, is another Little Gidding harmony, which was probably made for Prince Charles. It measures 29 × 20 inches, and is bound in purple velvet, and decorated with gold stamp-work of a similar kind. It was probably made about 1642, and now belongs to Captain Gaussen. The whole history of Little Gidding is most interesting; and, from a binding point of view, its existence during the reign of Charles I., and his kindly appreciation and patronage of it in the midst of all his own troubles, will always mark his reign as an important epoch in English bookbinding. Illustrations of many of the Little Gidding bindings are given in *Bibliographica*, part vi.

No particular binding seems to have been made during the period of the Commonwealth, at all events I have never been able to discover one in any of our large libraries; but, to make up for this, during the reign of Charles II. we have a profusion of royal bindings, many of which are of considerable beauty. The appointment of Samuel Mearne as royal bookbinder to Charles II. was in force from 1660 to 1683, and no doubt long before this Mearne was well known as a fine binder. There is a good deal of documentary evidence concerning Mearne, chiefly relating to bindings of Bibles and Prayer Books bound for the royal chapels, and others for the royal library at St. James's. He decorated his bindings in three styles, easily distinguishable from each other. Books bound in the first, or simplest, style are always covered with red morocco, and have a rectangular panel of gold lines stamped on each side, having at the outer corners fleurons, or the device of two C's, adossés, crowned, and partly enclosed within two laurel sprays. This device occurs commonly on Mearne's books. The backs of these volumes are often richly stamped with masses of small floral designs, and the lettering is remarkably clear and good. There are numbers of examples, both in our royal libraries and in the hands of private owners. Although they cannot be called very ornamental, they nevertheless are of excellent workmanship, and are always in good taste.

FIG. 18.—*Common Prayer. London, 1662. Charles II.*

The second division are bound in red or dark morocco, the boards being decorated with what is known as the "Cottage" design, usually having the crowned monogram in the centre, the remaining spaces being more or less filled with masses of small stamped work. The fillets and many of the flowers and ornaments are often picked out with black stain.

The third division are bound in red or black morocco, ornamented with mosaic work of coloured leathers—red, yellow, green, and white. Many of these books are so intricate in their design that they deserve special mention; but it may be said, generally, that the leading motive upon them is a modification or elaboration of the cottage design, so called because its leading motive is in the shape of the gable of a cottage roof.

One of the earliest bindings done for Charles is a copy of the Bible and Prayer Book, printed at Cambridge, 1660. It is a large book covered in red morocco, and has a rectangular panel and border, with the royal coat-of-arms in the centre, all richly decorated with small gold stamp-work. The binding is not very characteristic of Mearne, although it is often considered to be his work, and bears some of his stamps. Neither the crowned monogram which is used upon it, nor the crowned dove bearing an olive branch, is found on any other bindings by Mearne. The stamp of the dove with the olive branch is of course symbolical of Charles's return to the throne of his ancestors. The book may have been bound for special presentation to Charles on his accession to the throne.

In the royal library at Windsor are several specimens of Charles II. bindings. Among them are three copies of Charles I.'s *Eikon Basilike*. One of them is bound in dark blue morocco, with large royal coat-of-arms and supporters, crest and crown. Another in olive morocco is delicately stamped with arabesques, and the crowned initials C. R.; it has two silver clasps, with medallion portraits of Charles I. Another is bound in calf, having in the centre of each board a decorative portrait medallion of Charles I. in silver, within an ornamental border of figures and arabesques, having also engraved silver corner-pieces on the two front corners.

In the same library a copy of the Bible, 1660, and Taylor's *Rule of Conscience*, 1676, are bound respectively in black and red morocco, and are brilliant specimens of Samuel Mearne's work. The boards are covered with many irregular small panels, each closely filled with small stamped work. The Bible was lent to the Burlington Fine Arts Club in 1891, and is figured both in their Catalogue and in Mr. Holmes's book of the bookbindings at Windsor. A copy of the works of Charles I., 1662, now at Windsor, is a beautiful example of Samuel Mearne's inlaid work. It is bound in deep red morocco, with an inner panel marked with white leather. In the centre is the royal coat, with supporters and crest; and the remainder of the boards, especially the corners, are ornamented with elaborate inlays of green and yellow leather, and richly stamped in gold.

The British Museum is also rich in Charles II. bindings. The Common Prayer, printed in London in 1622, measuring $17\frac{1}{4} \times 11\frac{1}{2}$ inches, was bound for him in black morocco, elaborately inlaid, and stamped in gold (Fig. 18). A broad, yellow, rectangular panel encloses at the present time a stamp of the coat-of-arms of one of the Georges. This, of course, is a subsequent addition, and it is impossible to say for certain whether there was originally any stamp in the centre of the book or not; but probably there was a crowned initial. The inner sides and corners of this panel are ornamented with mosaics of white, red, and yellow leather, with gilded sprays and small stamps. The outer edges of the panel have at the top and bottom a cottage arrangement, filled in with small dotted scale ornament, and further decorated with red mosaic inlays, having gold stamps and sprays. A somewhat similar arrangement at the sides has scale patterns and red mosaics, and the crowned initials of the king are impressed at the roof angles. The gilt front edges of this volume are decorated with paintings of incidents chosen from the life of Christ, executed under the gold, and only visible when held in a certain position.

FIG. 19.—*A short View of the late Troubles in England, etc. Oxford, 1681. Charles II.*

A copy of the Book of Common Prayer, printed in London, 1669, is covered in red morocco, and bears upon each board a modification of the roofed pattern, stained black, and broken by curves at the upper and lower points and at the sides. In the centre, the crowned C's are enclosed in a small inner fillet, coloured black, and supplemented with very delicate arabesque stamped work in gold. The inner angles of the roof and sides are filled with scale patterns in dots. Above and below the centre-piece are bold leaf sprays. The corners and spaces throughout are filled with very close gold stamped arabesques, circles, and small flowers. It has an elaborate outer border of an enlarged scaled pattern filled with small stamps. The book is a very beautiful one, and is, in some ways, the finest specimen of Mearne's work existing. It has frequently been figured. Under the gilding on the front edges is a painting, having as its centre motive the design of the crowned C's and the laurel branches already mentioned. This method of painting under the gold, which appears to have been first done by an artist of the name of Fletcher, is frequently found on Mearne's bindings. The custom dropped into disuse after his time, until it was revived by Edwards of Halifax about a hundred years later.

A copy of the Scottish Laws and Acts of James I., Edinburgh, 1661, is covered in red morocco. It has in the centre a large irregular panel, inlaid in black morocco, bearing the royal coat-of-arms, crowned, within the Garter, and the initials C. II. R., the rest of the black panel being thickly gilded with ornamental sprays. There are large angle-pieces of yellow leather, richly stamped, and at the sides, upper, and lower edges of each board are urns carrying large branching sprays, with flowers inlaid in yellow and black leathers.

A short View of the late Troubles in England, Oxford, 1681 (Fig. 19), is bound in red morocco, and ornamented all over the boards with small, irregular panels, outlined by broad gold lines, and filled with mosaics of black and yellow leather, all ornamented thickly with small gold stamp-work. In the centre, on a black panel, are large ornamental initials, "C. R.," crowned. Although this binding has many points in common with Samuel Mearne's work, it is lacking in finish, and it is probably the work of his son Charles, who afterwards succeeded him as royal binder. A copy of Fox's *Book of Martyrs*, London, 1641, also bound in Mearne's fashion, bears upon its front edges, under the gilding, a portrait of the king in his coronation robes. It is figured in *Bibliographica*, part viii., and is signed "Fletcher."

FIG. 20.—*Bible. Cambridge, 1674. James II.*

There are in the British Museum two large volumes of an English Atlas, measuring 23 × 15 inches. The first of them bears the large ornamental initials C. R. crowned. It has a modification of the cottage design, arranged in an interlacing fillet of yellow leather, within which is a symmetrical arrangement of irregular panels, inlaid with black and yellow morocco, all richly edged and filled in with small gold stamped work, picked out with silver. The second volume is ornamented in a similar manner with inlays, but has not the outer border or the initials.

Although there are many of Mearne's bindings to be found in the large private libraries throughout England, probably the finest is that which belongs to the Earl of Crewe, at Crewe Hall. It covers a folio Book of Common Prayer, 1662, and bears the cottage design, outlined in yellow leather, with scale pattern. There are fine mosaics of red, yellow, and green leathers in the corners of the inner panel, covered with close gold stamp-work and floral sprays. The crowned C's are in the centre within an ornamental border, and outside the yellow panel are red and green mosaics, thickly covered with small gold work.

Mr. Almack, in his valuable *Bibliography of the King's Book* or *Eikon Basilike*, gives a plate of a binding that covers an edition of 1649, but which was bound for Charles II. by Samuel Mearne. It bears the royal coat-of-arms, with garter and crest, within a rectangular panel enriched with small gold stamps. It is in red morocco. Several of the editions of the *Eikon* bear the initials C. R. upon their covers, with other emblems, but it is most likely that these letters refer to the author rather than to the owner.

Mr. E. H. Lawrence lent to the Burlington Fine Arts Club Exhibition of Bookbindings an exquisite specimen of Samuel Mearne's work. It is a collection of anthems, with music, bound in dark blue morocco. It is elaborately stamped in gold, with a curved adaptation of the cottage design, closely filled in with masses of small gold work along the inner and outer edges. The crowned monogram, with laurel sprays, is in the centre of each of the sides, and it has a rich double border of scale patterns filled with gold stamped work.

In the library at Windsor are several bindings that were done for James II., but they are generally of a simple kind, bearing heraldic devices in the centre enclosed in rectangular panels of more or less elaboration. At the British Museum are some Jacobean bindings of a more ornamental kind. One of these, a Cambridge Bible of 1674, is bound in crimson velvet, and has rich silk ties with bullion fringe (Fig. 20). It is heavily embroidered in gold, silver, and coloured silks, and bears in the centre the crowned initials "J. R." enclosed in a strap border intertwined with rose sprays and other floral designs. In each of the corners is a cherub's head with wings. There are two volumes, each measuring 18 × 12 inches. Although, from the size of these books and the splendid colour, they are undoubtedly of imposing appearance, neither the design nor the workmanship can be considered of a high quality.

Belonging to the King's Library in the British Museum are two specimens, almost exactly alike except for their size, which may, for the present, be considered the finest that were done for James II. One of these is a Common Prayer, printed at Oxford in 1681. It is bound in red morocco, and has a black "cottage" fillet, broken at the angles and at each side. The crowned monogram "J. R.," with laurel spray, occurs in several places on the boards. The remaining spaces are closely filled with small gold stamped work, similar to that used by Samuel Mearne. The book is an unusually fat one, and bears upon its broad front edges, under the gold, the most elaborate painting I have found in such a position. It has the full coat-of-arms of England, with supporters, crown, and crest, enclosed in an elaborate border of flowers, cherubs, and ribbons. This painting is in remarkably fine condition, but, like all this class of work, the appearance of it depends very largely upon the manner in which it is displayed. The companion volume is a Bible of 1685. It is bound in an almost identical way; but the painting on the edge, although brighter, is not to be compared with it, either for size or excellence.

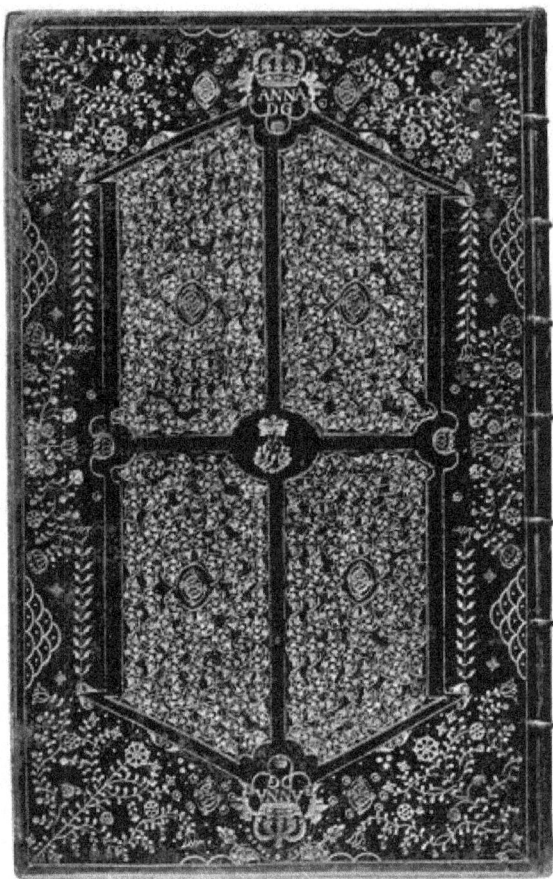

FIG. 21.—*Euclide. Oxford, 1705. Queen Anne.*

A note at the beginning, signed *G. Sarum*, says that this was the book which "lay before His Majesty above two years in the closet of his chappell," and afterwards it was the property of the Archbishop of Canterbury, and then of the Bishop himself.

At Windsor there is a small book bound for Mary of Modena in red morocco, with the royal coats of England and Este, crowned, and enclosed within a cordelière des veuves, the rest, with the field, being occupied with small panels ornamented in the Mearne fashion.

At the British Museum is a copy of Walter's Poems, printed in 1668, that was dedicated by him to the Duchess of York, with an autograph poem. It is bound in black morocco, and bears the arms of England, with a label, impaled with those of Este, with supporters, and surmounted with a prince's coronet. Above and below the coat-of-arms are curves and arabesques in dotted gold work, picked out with silver, all enclosed in a rectangular border of a Mearne pattern.

The bindings of William and Mary are not remarkable in any way, except for their peculiar arrangement of the quarterings of the royal coat. A fine copy of *Veues des belles maisons de France*, bound in red morocco, has in the centre a crowned shield within a Garter, the bearings being—first, the coat of England; second, the coat of Scotland; third, the coat of France; fourth, the coat of Ireland; over all the scutcheon of Nassau. In each corner is a handsome crowned monogram, "W. M." The volume is at Windsor. In the same library is a copy of the Statutes of the Order of the Garter, bound in dark blue morocco, and bearing in the centre, within a Mearne border, the royal coat-of-arms, crowned, with Garter. On the dexter side is the Cross of St. George; on the sinister side, the coat of England with the quarterings in their proper order.

FIG. 22.—*Ælfric. An English-Saxon Homily on the Birthday of St. Gregory. London, 1709. Queen Anne.*

In the British Museum are other bindings of William and Mary, but they are also of small importance from a decorative point of view. They often bear the crowned initials "W. R." enclosed in laurel sprays, and are ornamented with lines and small sprays in gold, mostly after the Mearne fashion. A copy of the *Memoirs of the Earl of Castlehaven*, London, 1681, has the coat arranged in the following curious manner: first, England; second, Scotland; third, Ireland; fourth, France, with scutcheon of Nassau over all. It almost seemed as if William considered that the coat of France had been borne long enough by English sovereigns, and it occupied the place of honour until he deposed it from that proud position; but I believe it was only upon his bookbindings that he took these liberties with the fleurs-de-lis.

The finest of Queen Anne's bindings at Windsor is a copy of Flamsteed, *Historia Cœlestis*, 1712. It is bound in red morocco, and has in the centre the full arms of England with supporters. The arms are quartered as follows: first and fourth, England and Scotland impaled; second, France; and third, Ireland; all within mitred panels, ornamented with small arabesques and floral sprays at the angles and sides. In the same library is also a binding with the monogram of William, Duke of Gloucester, son of Queen Anne, with a prince's coronet enclosed in a triple-bordered panel, with sprays and acorns.

In the British Museum the richest binding done for Queen Anne is on a copy of the English *Euclide*, Oxford, 1705 (Fig. 21). It is a large book, and the centre is occupied by a cottage design divided into four panels, each of which is thickly filled with small gold stamped work. At the upper and lower edges of the boards are the words "ANNA D. G.," under a royal crown, upheld by two cherubs; above which is a scroll bearing the words "VIVAT REGINA." The outer corners and the sides are filled with scale ornaments and floral sprays of a branching character.

Another volume bound for Queen Anne, in the British Museum, is *An English-Saxon Homily on the Birthday of St. Gregory*, by Ælfric, Archbishop of Canterbury, London, 1709 (Fig. 22). It is covered in red morocco, and stamped in gold with a cottage design, and bears the crowned monogram "A. R.," with laurel sprays and other small stamps scattered about. The designs on all these volumes of the later Stuart sovereigns have no very distinctive character, and, except where they are frank imitations of Mearne's work, they show little inventive power.

On the legislative union of England and Scotland in 1706, the first and fourth quarters of the royal coat bore the coats of England and Scotland impaled, the second quarter the coat of France, and the third that of Ireland. It is important to remember this change, as the first quarter continued to be used in the same way on Queen Anne's books and on those of her successors until 1801.

CHAPTER IV

GEORGE I.—GEORGE II.—GEORGE III.—GEORGE IV.—
WILLIAM IV.

On the succession to the English crown passing to the Hanoverian line, another important change was made in the royal coat of England. George I. substituted for the fourth quarter, which had been hitherto a repetition of the first, the arms of his family, Brunswick, impaling Luneburg, and in the base point the coat of Saxony, over all an escutcheon, charged with the crown of Charlemagne, as a badge of the office of High Treasurer of the Holy Roman Empire. George II. bore the same coat as did George III. up to 1801, when, on the legislative union of Great Britain and Ireland, the coat was officially altered to first and fourth England; second, Scotland; third, Ireland, with over all an escutcheon, bearing the arms of the royal dominions in Germany, ensigned with the electoral bonnet, which was again changed to the Hanoverian royal crown when Hanover was elevated to the rank of a kingdom in 1816. This last coat was used by George IV. and William IV., and, without the Hanoverian escutcheon, it is the present royal coat of England.

The bindings of George I. and George II. are generally much alike. There are good specimens of each at Windsor. They are generally in red morocco, with either coats-of-arms in the centre or monograms. At Windsor there is one bound in vellum, it is a manuscript *Report on States of Traytors*, 1717, and bears the full royal coat in the centre, enclosed in rectangular mitred borders, with delicate gold stamped work at the sides. In the British Museum is a finely stamped *Account of Conference concerning the Succession to the Crown*, 1719, very delicately and tastefully ornamented, having the coat-of-arms in the centre, with crowned initials at the corners, and delicate gold work of floral sprays and curves borrowed from Le Gascon, a great French binder.

FIG. 23.—*Account of what passed in a Conference concerning the Succession to the Crown, MS. George I.*

FIG. 24.—*Le Nouveau Testament. Amsterdam, 1718. George II.*

There are several of George II. bindings at Windsor, made for him when he was Prince of Wales. These generally bear the Prince of Wales' feathers as a chief motive, and they often have broad borders, much of the ornamentation of which contains stamps of crowns, sceptres, and birds, which are attributed to Eliot and Chapman. There are other inlaid bindings made for George II. which often have doublures. Some of these are figured in Mr. Holmes's *Bookbindings at Windsor.* Bindings of a similar kind that were made for Frederick Prince of Wales, and for his wife, the Princess Augusta, are also preserved at Windsor. These have always heraldic centres, and generally the broad Eliot and Chapman outer borders.

FIG. 25.—*Chandler. A Vindication of the Defence of Christianity.* London, 1728. George II.

FIG. 26.—*Common Prayer. Cambridge, 1760.*
Queen Charlotte.

For George III., both when Prince of Wales and King, books were bound with coloured inlays by Andreas Lande. There are specimens of his work both in the British Museum and at Windsor, they are not in particularly good taste. During the reign of George III. a remarkable English bookbinder worked in London. This was Roger Payne; and, although he himself does not seem to have bound any royal books, he strongly influenced many who did, more particularly Kalthœber, who bound many of the books in the King's Library at the British Museum. Although these bindings are by no means so good as their originals, they are a very great advance upon their immediate predecessors; and a delicately worked and effective instance covers a copy of the Gutenburg Bible now at the British Museum.

Another English binder of note, James Edwards of Halifax, also flourished in the reign of George III. This binder has not, I think, received sufficient appreciation, as he discovered an entirely new way of treating vellum by which it was rendered transparent. He painted designs on the under side of the vellum and bound his books with it, the result being that, if the vellum is clean on the outside, the protected painting underneath it is as fresh as when it was first done. A fine example of this curious work is on a copy of a Prayer Book, printed at Cambridge, 1760, which belonged to Charlotte of Mecklenburg, queen of George III. (Fig. 26). Her arms, in proper heraldic colours, are in the centre of the upper cover, enclosed by a blue and gold border of Etruscan design. At the lower edge is a miniature of a ruin in monotone, and at each side of the coat and above it are ornamental scrolls, with conventional flowers, birds, animals, and figures. On the lower cover is a central oval, with an allegorical figure in monotone, enclosed in a similar border to that on the upper cover, at each side of which are flowering trees in urns, birds, etc., and in each panel of the back is also a decorative design. Altogether this is the prettiest royal binding done at this period. It has the crowned initials "C. R." painted in silver inside the upper cover, and on the front edge, in an oval, is a painting of the Resurrection under the gold. Between this and the edges, painted for James II., there were no books adorned in this way for royal owners.

FIG. 27.—*Portfolio containing the Royal Letter concerning the King's Library. George IV.*

The bindings done for George IV., at Windsor, are generally bound in red morocco, with heraldic centres and broad borders, sometimes inlaid with coloured leathers. The borders are sometimes like those used by Eliot and Chapman, and sometimes conventional patterns. A good example in the British Museum is on the cover of the letter written to Lord Liverpool by the king in 1823, concerning the gift of his father's library to the nation. A copy of the Book of Common Prayer, which belonged to William IV., and is now at Windsor, is bound in blue morocco. It bears in the centre the star of the Order of the Garter, within a crowned Garter, dependent from which is an anchor, and at the sides "G. R. III." There are anchors in the corners, and a decorative outer border. The generality of the books belonging to him have the usual heraldic centres, within borders designed in more or less good taste. The king presented to the British Museum, and signed with his own name, an *Inventory of the Crown Plate*, 1832. It is bound by William Clark, and bears in the centre the full royal coat-of-arms, and has a handsome rectangular border of triple gold lines, broken at each side by bold arabesque ornaments.

EPILOGUE

In the foregoing detailed descriptions I have included only the work of English binders. There are, however, many books existing that have been bound for English royal personages abroad. Instances of these occur notably for Henry VIII., Elizabeth, James I., Henrietta Maria, Henrietta Anna, Charles II., the Chevalier St. George, and Cardinal York. It will be noticed that generally the ornamentation of English royal books is heraldic, and that crowned initials are constantly used from the time of Henry VIII. to William IV. To understand the royal coat-of-arms of England it is necessary, at all events, to note the larger rearrangements of the various quarterings, which on the Tudor bindings were simply France and England, quarterly. The two great changes took place on the accession of the Stuart line, when the coats of Scotland and England were introduced; and on the accession of the Hanoverian line, when the family coat of the Guelphs was introduced. There are several minor alterations and additions, but these I have mentioned as they have occurred, and the only other important change to remember is concerning the supporters. From the time of Henry VII. until 1528 these were a dragon and a greyhound, and from that time until Elizabeth they were a lion and a dragon. Since the time of James I. they have been a lion and unicorn. Badges are constantly found on Tudor and early Stuart bindings. They are the well-known ones of Tudor origin—the double rose, portcullis, pomegranate, fleur-de-lis, and falcon. The fleur-de-lis remains longest of these. The Prince of Wales' feathers is commonly found on books from the time of Edward VI.

The styles of bindings used by these great royal houses have also characteristics common to each of them. The bindings of the Tudor period are most diversified in styles, and the majority of the leather books are either bound by Thomas Berthelet, royal binder to Henry VIII., and his successors, or in his style. Under Elizabeth, the Italian fashion of double boards, the upper of which is pierced, was used for very choice work. Berthelet took his inspiration originally from Italian models, but shortly developed a style of his own. Vellum was much used in connection with gold stamped work, the first use of which in England is credited to this binder.

Order of the Coronation of George III. and Queen Charlotte.
London, 1761. George III.

The bindings of the early Stuart period may be considered remarkable for the extensive use of what are called semées, successive and symmetrical impressions from small stamps powdered over the sides of the book; and the stamped velvet work done at Little Gidding is one of the glories of the reign of Charles I.

Samuel Mearne was royal binder to Charles II., and many of his bindings are of great beauty. His influence on English bookbinding remained for a very long time, weakening gradually, until superseded by the newer style introduced by Roger Payne.

In the time of George III. there was some improvement in royal bindings due to the imitators of Roger Payne, another binder, whose influence was strongly felt after his death. Eliot and Chapman, during the eighteenth century, introduced the use of broad borders with small stamps, among which are frequently found crowns and sceptres; and many of these are found on royal bindings.

Names of many royal binders, from early times, are preserved in various records, but there is considerable uncertainty about the work of most of them; and, although many lists exist of books bound for certain kings by certain workmen, very few of them have been identified. From the constant appearance of personal badges of different kinds, it may be considered likely that, especially among the earlier sovereigns, considerable personal interest has been taken in the covering of their books. We even find the livery colours of the Tudors—green and white—duly used on some of their bindings; and the prevalence of red and blue, the livery colours of the Hanoverian line, is common enough among the Georgian bindings.

www.ingramcontent.com/pod-product-compliance
Lightning Source LLC
Chambersburg PA
CBHW031148090426
42738CB00008B/1260